HIPAA Compliance Handbook 2003

Patricia I. Carter, J.D.
Gray, Plant, Mooty, Mooty & Bennett, P.A.

1185 Avenue of the Americas, New York, NY 10036
www.aspenpublishers.com

"This publication is designed to provide accurate and authoritative information in regard to the Subject Matter covered. It is sold with the understanding that the publisher is not engaged in rendering legal, accounting, or other professional service. If legal advice or other expert assistance is required, the services of a competent professional person should be sought."

From a Declaration of Principles jointly adopted by a Committee of the American Bar Association and a Committee of Publishers and Associations.)

Library of Congress Cataloging-in-Publication data available on request

Copyright © 2003 by Aspen Publishers, Inc.
A Wolters Kluwer Company
www.aspenpublishers.com
All rights reserved.

Editorial Services: Amy L. Frevert
Printing and Manufacturing: Susan Ballos

All rights reserved. No part of this publication may be reproduced; stored in or introduced into a retrieval system now known or to be invented; transmitted in any form or by any means (electronic, mechanical, recording, or otherwise); or used for advertising or promotional purposes, general distribution, creating new collective works, or for resale, without prior written permission of the copyright owner and publisher. An exception to this policy is the reproduction of forms, handouts, or procedures contained herein solely for use within the site-of-purchase facility. Submit written permission requests to Aspen Publishers, Inc., Health Law Department, 200 Orchard Ridge Drive, Suite 200, Gaithersburg, Maryland 20878.

Orders: (800) 638-8437
Customer Service: (800) 234-1660

ISBN: 0-7355-3937-5

Printed in the United States of America

1 2 3 4 5

About Aspen Publishers

Aspen Publishers, headquartered in New York City, is a leading information provider for attorneys, business professionals, and law students. Written by preeminent authorities, our products consist of analytical and practical information covering both U.S. and international topics. We publish in the full range of formats, including updated manuals, books, periodicals, CDs, and online products.

Our proprietary content is complemented by 2,500 legal databases, containing over 11 million documents, available through our Loislaw division. Aspen Publishers also offers a wide range of topical legal and business databases linked to Loislaw's primary material. Our mission is to provide accurate, timely, and authoritative content in easily accessible formats, supported by unmatched customer care.

How to Order

To order any Aspen Publishers title, or to reinstate your manual update service, please call: 1-800-638-8437.

For Customer Care issues, please call 1-800-234-1660, fax 1-800-901-9075, or email CustomerCare@aspenpublishers.com

Aspen Publishers
A Wolters Kluwer company
1185 Avenue of the Americas
New York, NY 10036

SUBSCRIPTION NOTICE

This Aspen Publishers product is updated on a periodic basis with supplements to reflect important changes in the subject matter. If you purchased this product directly from Aspen Publishers, we have already recorded your subscription for the update service.

If, however, you purchased this product from a bookstore and wish to receive future updates and revised or related volumes billed separately with a 30-day examination review, please contact our Customer Care Department at 1-800-234-1660, or send your name, company name (if applicable), address, and the title of the product to:

Aspen Publishers
A Division of Aspen Publishers, Inc.
7201 McKinney Circle
Frederick, MD 21704

Table of Contents

	Page
PREFACE	vii
I. HEALTH INFORMATION AND ADMINISTRATIVE SIMPLIFICATION	1
A. Background: Administrative Simplification	1
B. To Whom Will the Regulations Apply?	2
1. Covered Entities	2
2. Outsourcing	2
3. Dual Applicability	3
C. Compliance Dates	3
1. Transaction Standards	3
2. Privacy Regulations	3
3. Security Regulations	3
4. Special Rule for Small Health Plans	4
D. Penalties	4
1. Civil Penalties	5
2. Criminal Penalties	5
II. ELECTRONIC TRANSACTIONS, IDENTIFIERS, AND CODE SETS REGULATIONS	7
III. PRIVACY REGULATIONS	9
A. Purpose and General Principles	9
1. The Main Principle	9
2. What Is Protected Health Information?	9
3. Preemption	12
4. Scalability and Flexibility	13
B. Individual Rights	13
1. Notice of Privacy Practices	13
2. Access	17
3. Amendments	18
4. Accounting of Disclosures	19
5. Restrictions and Confidential Communications	20
6. No Private Right of Action	20
C. Use and Disclosure of PHI	21
1. Required and Permitted Uses and Disclosures	21

	Page
2. Treatment, Payment, and Health Care Operations	21
3. Opt Out Approach	23
4. Uses and Disclosures for Which No Permission Is Required	25
5. All Other Purposes—Authorization	31
D. Special Applications of the Rules Relating to Uses and Disclosures	34
1. Fundraising	34
2. Marketing	34
3. Mental Health Records and Psychotherapy Notes	35
4. Underwriting	36
5. Special Categories of Individuals	36
6. Incidental Disclosures	38
E. Administrative Requirements	39
1. Designation of Privacy Official and Contact Person	39
2. Training	39
3. Safeguards	40
4. Complaints	40
5. Sanctions	41
6. Duty to Mitigate	41
7. Refraining from Intimidating or Retaliatory Acts	41
8. Waiver of Rights	41
9. Policies and Procedures	42
10. Documentation	42
F. Business Associates	43
1. Who is a Business Associate	43
2. Business Associate Contracts–Contents	45
3. Business Associate Contracts–Deadline	46
4. Enforcement	47
G. Other Key Concepts	47
1. Organizational Structure	47
2. Minimum Necessary	48
3. Verification	49
IV. PROPOSED SECURITY REGULATIONS	**51**
A. Administrative Procedures	52
1. Certification	52
2. Chain of Trust Partner Agreement	52
3. Contingency Plan	52
4. Formal Mechanism for Processing Records	52
5. Information Access Control	53
6. Internal Audit	53
7. Personnel Security	53
8. Security Configuration Management	54
9. Security Incident Procedures	54
10. Security Management Process	54
11. Termination Procedures	55
12. Training	55
B. Physical Safeguards	56
1. Assigned Security Responsibility	56
2. Media Controls	56
3. Physical Access Controls	56
4. Policy/Guideline on Workstation Use	57

		Page
5. Secure Workstation Location		57
6. Security Awareness Training		57
C. Technical Data Security Services		58
1. Access Control		58
2. Audit Controls		58
3. Authorization Control		58
4. Data Authentication		58
5. Entity Authentication		59
D. Technical Security Mechanisms		59
E. Electronic Signatures		60
F. Integration of Privacy and Security		60
V. EMPLOYER-SPONSORED HEALTH PLANS		**61**
A. Applicability		61
B. Covered Plans		61
C. Transaction Standards		61
D. Privacy Regulations		62
E. Security Regulations		65
Appendix A: Sample Business Associate Contract		67
Appendix B: Sample Plan Document Amendment		73
Appendix C: State-by-State Guide to Medical Privacy Statutes		75
Appendix D: ABC Health Care System Privacy Policies and Procedures		127
About the Author		137

Preface

Pursuant to the Health Insurance Portability and Accountability Act of 1996 (HIPAA), the Department of Health and Human Services (DHHS) has issued three key sets of federal regulations regarding health information. These regulations are the subject of this book. At the time of this writing, some of these regulations remain a "moving target." Additional proposed regulations have been issued and modifications are expected. The standards for electronic transactions and code sets are still evolving—DHHS issued proposed changes in May 2002. The proposed security regulations were originally published in August 1998. DHHS has stated that the final security regulations are not expected to differ significantly from those proposed, but at the time of this writing, the final regulations have not been published.

In the midst of these evolving standards, health care providers, health plans, and clearinghouses covered by these HIPAA regulations must continue to move forward to achieve compliance by the applicable compliance dates. This book is based on the status of the HIPAA regulations as of September 2002. The reader is reminded to refer to the final version of each regulation for compliance purposes. The regulations are available at the DHHS Administrative Simplification Web site: aspe.os.dhhs.gov/admnsimp/.

This book is not intended as legal advice or a substitute for a thorough study of the regulations, but to serve as a tool to assist the reader in understanding these complex requirements.

I. HEALTH INFORMATION AND ADMINISTRATIVE SIMPLIFICATION

A. Administrative Simplification

Following the demise of the Clinton administration's Task Force on National Health Care Reform in the early 1990s, Congress decided to take a more incremental approach to health care reform. The Health Insurance Portability and Accountability Act of 1996 (HIPAA)[1] was enacted on August 21, 1996, as a major part of this initiative. The initial focus of HIPAA was on the problem of the uninsured, and HIPAA tackled the issue of the portability of health insurance coverage and made it easier for employees to retain health coverage when they changed jobs or had changes in family status. Other main purposes of HIPAA were to combat waste, fraud, and abuse in the health care system, and to simplify the administration of health insurance.[2]

The section of HIPAA called Administrative Simplification[3] is the focus of this book. The Administrative Simplification provisions were added to HIPAA because health care providers and health plans wanted a single federal standard for the format of electronic health care claims to facilitate electronic data interchange. Hundreds of formats for claims transactions were then in use and this lack of standardization was seen as impeding the move away from paper transactions to a more efficient electronic exchange of information. This standardization was intended to improve the Medicare and Medicaid programs, and the efficiency and effectiveness of the health care system generally.[4]

Congress was willing to establish electronic standards for claims and other common transactions, but had concerns about the confidentiality and security of individuals' health care information. In a computerized environment in which sensitive medical records could be widely disseminated very easily, and where breaches of confidentiality could happen on a previously inconceivable scale, additional privacy and security measures were needed.[5] As a result, to balance the standardization that would increase the volume of electronic health care information, Congress added provisions to the HIPAA legislation to provide increased privacy and security protections for individually identifiable health care information.

HIPAA requires the Department of Health and Human Services (DHHS) to develop and implement standards for the electronic transmission of certain health information and to protect the privacy and security of individually identifiable health information.[6] To this end, DHHS has issued three sets of federal regulations (the "Administrative Simplification Regulations").

- *Transactions*: Standards for the content and format of certain electronic transactions, including standard code sets (the "Transaction Standards")[7]
- *Privacy*: Regulations safeguarding the privacy of an individual's health care information, and establishing certain individual rights with respect to that information (the "Privacy Regulations")[8]
- *Security*: Standards for assuring the confidentially, integrity, and accessibility of electronic health information (the "Security Regulations")[9]

---

[1] Pub. L. No. 104-191, 110 Stat. 1936 (codified in scattered sections of 18, 26, 29, and 42 U.S.C.).
[2] Pub. L. No. 104-191, preface, 110 Stat. at 1936.
[3] Pub. L. No. 104-191, Title II, Subpt. F.
[4] Pub. L. No. 104-191, § 261.
[5] 65 Fed. Reg. 82474.
[6] Pub. L. No. 104-191, §§ 263, 264 (codified at 42 U.S.C. 1320d-2 to 1320d-8).
[7] 45 C.F.R. Parts 160 and 162; 65 Fed. Reg. 50311 (Aug. 17, 2000); 65 Fed. Reg. 70507 (Nov. 24, 2000)(correcting certain minor errors); 67 Fed. Reg. 38050 (May 31, 2002)(proposed changes).
[8] 45 C.F.R. Parts 160 and 164; 65 Fed. Reg. 82462 (Dec. 28, 2000); 66 Fed. Reg. 12434 (Feb.26, 2001) (changing compliance date); 67 Fed. Reg. 14776 (Apr. 14, 2002)(elimination of consent requirement and other changes).
[9] 45 C.F.R. Part 142 (proposed); 63 Fed. Reg. 43242 (Aug. 12, 1998)(proposed).

Section I of this book will address some issues common to all three of the Administrative Simplification Regulations, then Sections II–IV will discuss each set of regulations in more detail. Section V will address the special issues applicable to group health plans.

B. To Whom Do the Administrative Simplification Regulations Apply?

1. Covered Entities

The Administrative Simplification Regulations apply to the following three types of health care entities (the "covered entities").[10]

a. Health Plans. Health plan means an individual or group plan that provides, or pays the cost of medical care. These include public and private plans offered, for example, through health insurers, health maintenance organizations (HMOs), Medicare, Medicaid, and most group health plans (whether insured or self-insured). There is an exception for a group health plan that has fewer than 50 participants and is administered by the employer that sponsors the plan.

b. Health Care Clearinghouses. A health care clearinghouse is a public or private entity, such as a billing service, repricing company, or value-added network that either: (i) processes or facilitates the processing of health information received from another entity in a nonstandard format or containing nonstandard data content into a standard transaction; or (ii) receives a standard transaction from another entity and processes or facilitates the processing of health information into a nonstandard format or nonstandard data content for the receiving entity.

Although a clearinghouse is a covered entity, it is generally also a business associate of a provider or health plan. The discussion of clearinghouses in this book is generally limited to their role as business associate.

c. Health Care Providers. A health care provider is a covered entity if two tests are satisfied. The provider must meet the HIPAA definition of "health care provider" and must conduct certain electronic transactions.

"Health care provider" is broadly defined as a provider of medical or health services described under Medicare Part A or Part B (which encompasses most typical health care services), or any other person or organization that furnishes, bills, or is paid for health care in the normal course of business.

Whether a provider is a covered entity also depends on its conduct of certain transactions, as follows:

(i) Under the Transaction Standards and Privacy Regulations, any provider who chooses to <u>electronically</u> transmit or receive any of the enumerated standard transactions (e.g., transmitting or receiving billing/encounter information) is a covered entity. *See* Section II for a list of these transactions.
(ii) Under the Security Regulations, as proposed, a provider who electronically transmits or receives health information <u>or</u> who electronically maintains health information used in an electronic transmission between health care entities is a covered entity. This difference in application of the Security Regulations compared to the Privacy Regulations may be eliminated when the Security Regulations become final.

2. Outsourcing

A covered entity that uses an outside organization to perform some or all of its covered functions (i.e., the functions that make it a covered entity) remains a covered entity. For

---

[10] 42 U.S.C. § 1320d-1(a); 45 C.F.R. §§ 160.102 - 160.103 (Transaction Standards and Privacy Regulations); 45 C.F.R. §§ 142.102; 142.302 (Security Regulations, proposed).

example, a provider that uses a billing service, and an employer-sponsored health plan that uses a third-party administrator (TPA) remain covered entities. HIPAA implementation will be affected by such outsourcing, but the covered entity remains responsible for compliance and must assure that all applicable regulatory requirements are met.

3. Dual Applicability

Providers will often find that they are subject to the HIPAA Administrative Simplification Regulations both as providers and as health plans, because they are covered health care providers who also sponsor group health plans for their employees. Providers need to be aware of this dual compliance track, and that the application of the regulations to providers and health plans differs in certain respects.

C. Compliance Dates

Compliance with each set of the Administrative Simplification Regulations is required 24 months after the effective date of the final regulations, which is 60 days after publication in the *Federal Register*.

1. Transaction Standards

The final Transaction Standards were published August 17, 2000, and compliance is required by October 16, 2002 (or October 16, 2003, if an extension is requested under the Administrative Simplification Compliance Act).[11]

2. Privacy Regulations[12]

Final Privacy Regulations were published December 28, 2000. The Bush administration, after taking office in January 2001, reopened the Privacy Regulations for a new 30-day comment period, through March 30, 2001. The new administration then allowed the Privacy Regulations to take effect but announced that they would propose changes to address certain "unintended consequences" of the regulations. The revised effective date became April 14, 2001, and the compliance date is April 14, 2003. Proposed changes were issued March 27, 2002, and after a short comment period, final regulations modifying the Privacy Regulations were published August 14, 2002.[13] These modifications did not change the April 14, 2002 compliance date.

3. Security Regulations

The Security Regulations have been delayed numerous times. At present, DHHS is estimating that final regulations will be issued in October 2002. If so, the compliance date will be in December 2004.

---

[11] 45 C.F.R. § 162.900 (setting the original October 16, 2002, compliance date). On December 27, 2001, President Bush signed into law the Administrative Simplification Compliance Act (ASCA), Pub. L. 107-105, which permits an extension of one year, until October 16, 2003, for compliance with the HIPAA Transaction Standards. The extension is not automatic and must be applied for by October 15, 2002. With this extension, health plans, providers, and clearinghouses will have more time, if needed, to develop software, build systems, perform tests, and successfully implement the HIPAA Transaction Standards. This extension does not affect small health plans for which the compliance date remains October 16, 2003.

[12] 45 C.F.R. § 164.534 (as amended by 66 Fed. Reg. 12433 (Feb. 26, 2001)).

[13] 67 Fed. Reg. 14776.

4. Special Rule for Small Health Plans

For small health plans (i.e., health plans with $5 million or less in annual receipts), an additional 12 months is added to each regulatory compliance date.[14] DHHS has issued the following guidance in interpreting what receipts to use to determine whether a health plan qualifies as a small health plan.[15]

Health Plans: Health plans that file certain federal tax returns and report receipts on those returns should use the following guidance provided by the Small Business Administration at 13 C.F.R. § 121.104 to calculate annual receipts. Receipts means "total income" (or in the case of a sole proprietorship, "gross income") plus "cost of goods sold" as these terms are defined or reported on Internal Revenue Service ("IRS") federal tax return forms; Form 1120 for corporations; Form 1120S for Subchapter S corporations; Form 1065 for partnerships; and Form 1040, Schedule F, for farms or Schedule C for sole proprietorships). However, the term "receipts" excludes net capital gains or losses, taxes collected for and remitted to a taxing authority if included in gross or total income, proceeds from the transactions between a concern and its domestic or foreign affiliates (if also excluded from gross or total income on a consolidated return filed with the IRS), and amounts collected for another by a travel agent, real estate agent, advertising agent, conference management service provider, freight forwarder, or customs broker.

In calculating receipts under this guidance, health plans should use the definitions and process described at 13 C.F.R. § 121.104(a)(2)–(3) and § 121.104(b).

Generally, group health plans will not fall into the above category, but should be analyzed according to the rules below.

Group Health Plans: These health plans, which include ERISA group health plans sponsored by an employer, should use "proxy" measures to determine their annual receipts, as follows:

Fully insured health plans should use the amount of total premiums that they paid for health insurance benefits during the plan's last full fiscal year.

Self-insured health plans, both funded and unfunded, should use the total amount paid for health care claims by the employer, plan sponsor, or benefit fund, as applicable to their circumstances, on behalf of the plan during the plan's last full fiscal year.

Combination health plans: Those health plans that provide health benefits through a mix of purchased insurance and self-insurance should combine the proxy measures to determine their total annual receipts. That is, the health plan would add the insurance premiums for the insured portion and the claims paid for the self-insured portion to determine the total "annual receipts."

For an employer who is the sponsor of group health plans, a key aspect of the above calculation is determining how many separate health plans (i.e., how many covered entities) comprise the benefits offered to employees. Employers should refer to their annual Form 5500 filing for this information.

D. Penalties

Civil and criminal penalties for failure to comply with HIPAA are set forth in the statute.

---

[14] 45 C.F.R. § 160.103; 45 C.F.R. § 162.900; 45 C.F.R. § 164.534. The compliance date for the Transactions Standards for small health plans is already October 16, 2003, so no extension request under ASCA is required, and that date cannot be further extended.

[15] Guidance provided in Sept. 2002 by the Centers for Medicare and Medicaid Services (CMS) of DHHS. *Available at* http://cmshhs.custhelp.com/cgi-bin/cmshhs.cfg/php/enduser/std_adp.php?p_faqid=1183&p_created=1031601197.

1. Civil Penalties[16]

Noncompliance with the Administrative Simplification Regulations may result in maximum penalties of up to $100 per violation, with a maximum of $25,000 for all violations of an identical requirement by the same person in a calendar year.

2. Criminal Penalties[17]

HIPAA also establishes a fine of up to $50,000 and/or imprisonment for up to one year for any person who knowingly obtains or discloses individually identifiable health information in violation of the Administrative Simplification Regulations. If such offenses are committed under false pretenses, the penalty may be increased to up to $100,000 and/or imprisonment for up to five years. If the offense is committed with the intent to sell, transfer, or use individually identifiable health information for commercial advantage, personal gain, or malicious harm, the penalty is a fine of up to $250,000 and/or imprisonment for up to 10 years.

In addition to these penalties in the HIPAA statute, the Administrative Simplification Compliance Act provides that a covered entity that is not in compliance with the Transaction Standards by October 16, 2002 (or October 16, 2003, if an extension is obtained), is subject to exclusion from participation in the Medicare program, at the discretion of the Secretary of DHHS.[18]

The DHHS Office of Civil Rights is charged with enforcing the Privacy Regulations.[19] A separate enforcement regulation is to be issued in 2002 to provide more details about DHHS's approach to compliance and enforcement.

---

[16] Pub. L. 104-191, § 262(a) (codified at 42 U.S.C. § 1320d-5).
[17] Pub. L. 104-191, § 262(a) (codified at 42 U.S.C. § 1320d-6).
[18] Pub. L. 107-105.
[19] 65 Fed. Reg. 82381 (Dec. 28, 2000).

II. ELECTRONIC TRANSACTIONS, IDENTIFIERS, AND CODE SETS REGULATIONS

The core of HIPAA Administrative Simplification is the standardization of common electronic transactions, identifiers, and code sets. When HIPAA was enacted, health plans and health care providers were struggling to move toward automating certain common transactions, because electronic data interchange (EDI) was believed to be faster and more cost effective than paper-based transactions. One of the obstacles to EDI in health care was the fact that there were hundreds of custom formats for these transactions and little standardization. Congress added the Administrative Simplification provisions to HIPAA to address this problem. Under the HIPAA Transaction Standards, health plans must be prepared to accept the most common electronic transactions in new standardized formats, using standardized identifiers and codes. Providers may continue to conduct such transactions on paper, but if the transactions are conducted electronically, the standards must be followed.[1]

A complete and detailed description of the Transaction Standards is beyond the scope of this book, but a summary of the key provisions is provided below.

HIPAA defines a "transaction" as the "exchange of information between two parties to carry out financial or administrative activities related to health care."[2] In August 2000, final regulations for the content and format of the most common transactions (the first "standard transactions") were published.[3] Currently, standards have been established for the following eight health care-related standard transactions.

1. Health claims and equivalent encounter information
2. Health plan eligibility
3. Referral certification and authorization
4. Health care claim status
5. Health plan enrollments and disenrollments
6. Health care payment and remittance advice
7. Health plan premium payments
8. Coordination of benefits

Standards for additional transactions are expected to be issued at a later date.

HIPAA also requires the development of unique identifiers for individuals, employers, health plans, and health care providers. Congress has put the individual identifier on hold; the other identifiers are in various stages of development at this time.[4] The regulations also establish standard code sets, which are the codes to be used in the standard transactions to convey key information. Generally, these code sets are those already adopted by the health care system, such as ICD9-CM diagnosis codes and CPT-4 and HCPCS service codes.[5]

The general rule is that if a covered entity conducts one of these listed transactions with another covered entity (or within the same covered entity), using electronic media,[6] the covered entity must conduct the transaction as a standard transaction.[7] The standards may not be modified by the covered entity engaged in the transaction. No "local codes" or other customized variations are permitted.

---

[1] 45 C.F.R. §§ 160.923–160.930.
[2] 45 C.F.R. § 160.103.
[3] 65 Fed. Reg. 50311. *See also* proposed changes at 67 Fed. Reg. 38050 (May 31, 2002) (making required technical changes) and 67 Fed. Reg. 38044 (May 31, 2002) (modifying the required code set for prescription drugs).
[4] *See* aspe.os.dhhs.gov/admnsimp/pubsched.htm for updated information.
[5] 45 C.F.R. Part 162, subpart J.
[6] "Electronic media" means the mode of electronic transmission. It includes the Internet, Extranet, leased lines, dial-up lines, private networks, and those transmissions that are physically moved from one location to another using magnetic tape, disk, or compact disk media. 45 CFR § 162.103. Fax imaging and voice response transmissions are not subject to the HIPAA transactions standards.
[7] 45 CFR § 162.923 (a). DHHS Administration Simplification. FAQ 12/28/2000.

The following additional rules apply to health plans. (1) If an entity requests a health plan to conduct a transaction as a standard transaction, the health plan must do so. (2) A health plan may not delay or reject a transaction, or attempt to adversely affect the other entity or the transaction, because the transaction is a standard transaction. (3) A health plan may not reject a standard transaction on the basis that it contains data elements not needed or used by the health plan (for example, coordination of benefits information). (4) A health plan may not offer an incentive for a health care provider to conduct a transaction as a direct data entry transaction. (5) A health plan that operates as a clearinghouse, or requires an entity to use a clearinghouse to receive, process, or transmit a standard transaction may not charge fees or costs in excess of the fees or costs for normal telecommunications that the entity incurs when it directly transmits, or receives, a standard transaction to or from a health plan.[8]

A health plan must also meet each of the following requirements regarding code sets: (1) accept and promptly process any standard transaction that contains codes that are valid (as defined by these regulations); and (2) keep code sets for the current billing period (and appeals periods still open to processing under the terms of the health plan's coverage).[9]

The HIPAA Implementation Guides contain detailed implementation specifications for each standard transaction and have been provided to assist covered entities with developing software to comply with the Transaction Standards.[10] There is a separate Implementation Guide for each of the standard transactions. These Implementation Guides are very detailed and each is several hundred pages long. They may be downloaded from the Internet and are essential to implementation of the Transaction Standards.[11]

Those parties with whom a covered entity exchanges information in a HIPAA standard transaction are referred to as trading partners. Trading partners may enter into agreements regarding this exchange or transfer of information, but that agreement may not attempt to circumvent the Transaction Standards by establishing alternatives to the HIPAA-mandated format, content, identifiers, or code sets.[12]

---

[8] 45 CFR § 162.925 (a). In addition, if a health plan receives a standard transaction and coordinates benefits with another health plan (or another payor), it must store the coordination of benefits data it needs to forward the standard transaction to the other health plan (or other payer). 45 C.F.R. § 162.925 (b).
[9] 45 C.F.R. § 162.925 (c).
[10] See 45 C.F.R. § 162.920.
[11] See www.wpc-edi.com/hipaa/HIPAA_40.asp.
[12] 45 C.F.R. § 162.915.

III. PRIVACY REGULATIONS

A. Purpose and General Principles

The Privacy Regulations provide the first comprehensive federal protection for the privacy of health care information and will have a profound effect on the operations of covered entities. The Privacy Regulations control the internal uses and the external disclosures of health information. The Privacy Regulations also create certain individual patient rights, establish administrative requirements for the covered entities, and mandate that covered entities enter into contracts with their business associates to maintain protection of health information that is shared. DHHS explained the purpose of the Privacy Regulations this way.

> This regulation has three major purposes: (1) to protect and enhance the rights of consumers by providing them access to their health information and controlling the inappropriate use of that information; (2) to improve the quality of health care in the U.S. by restoring trust in the health care system among consumers, health care professionals, and the multitude of organizations and individuals committed to the delivery of care; and (3) to improve the efficiency and effectiveness of health care delivery by creating a national framework for health privacy protection that builds on efforts by states, health systems, and individual organizations and individuals.[1]

1. The Main Principle

Under the Privacy Regulations, covered entities may not use or disclose an individual's "protected health information" without permission of the individual, except as permitted or required by the regulations. Covered entities must reasonably safeguard protected health information from any intentional or unintentional use or disclosure that is in violation of the regulations.[2]

"Reasonable safeguards" does not mean protection from any and all potential risks; the determination is based on the particular facts and circumstances, including the financial and administrative burdens of any safeguards. (For example, a hospital is not required to remodel its facility to eliminate semi-private rooms.)

2. What Is Protected Health Information?

a. Definition. The type of information protected under the Privacy Regulations is called "protected health information" or "PHI." It is broadly defined as individually identifiable information, including demographic information, related to the past, present, or future physical or mental health or condition, the provision of health care to an individual, or the past, present, or future payment for such health care, that is created or received by a covered entity. The form of the PHI is irrelevant, and may be oral or recorded in any medium, including electronic data, paper records, or any other form.[3] The term "individual" is used in the Privacy Regulations and this book to refer to the person who is the subject of this PHI.

b. De-Identified Information. PHI must either identify the individual or there must be a reasonable basis to believe that the information can be used to identify the individual.[4] "De-identified information" is not PHI and not protected by the Privacy Regulation. This concept of de-identification is of great practical significance, because to the extent de-identified infor-

---

[1] 65 Fed. Reg. 84263.
[2] 45 C.F.R. § 164.504.
[3] 45 C.F.R. §§ 160.103; 164.501.
[4] 45 C.F.R. § 164.501.

mation can be used or disclosed in lieu of PHI, none of the complex requirements of the Privacy Regulations apply.

Information may be de-identified by either of two methods—the statistical approach and the safe harbor approach.[5] The statistical approach requires that a person with appropriate knowledge and experience of generally accepted statistical methods for rendering information not individually identifiable apply those methods and principles and determine that the risk is very small that the information could be used, alone or in combination with other reasonably available information, by an anticipated recipient to identify an individual who is a subject of the information. The expert must document the methods used and the results of this analysis.[6]

The safe harbor approach requires that the following data elements identifying the individual (or relatives, employers, or household members of the individual) be removed (provided the covered entity does not have actual knowledge that the remaining information could be used alone or in combination with other information to identify an individual who is a subject of the information):

- Names;
- All geographic subdivisions smaller than a state, including street address, city, county, precinct, zip code, and equivalent codes. The first three digits of the zip code may be retained if certain conditions are met (i.e., the zip code area is not too sparsely populated);
- All elements of dates (except year) for dates directly related to an individual including birth date, admission date, discharge date, date of death, and all ages over 89 and all elements of dates (including year) indicative of such age, except that such ages and elements may be aggregated into a single category of age 90 or older;
- Telephone numbers;
- Fax numbers;
- E-mail addresses;
- Social security numbers;
- Medical record numbers;
- Health plan beneficiary numbers;
- Account numbers;
- Certificate/license numbers;
- Vehicle identifiers and serial numbers, including license plate numbers;
- Device identifiers and serial numbers;
- Web addresses—Universal Resource Locators (URLs);
- Internet Protocol (IP) address numbers;
- Biometric identifiers, including finger and voice prints;
- Full face photographic images and any comparable images; and
- Any other unique identifying number, characteristic, or code (except a re-identification code).

A covered entity may assign a code or other means of record identification to allow re-identification of de-identified information, provided that the re-identification code (or other means of re-identification) is not derived from or related to information about the individual or capable of being used to identify the individual, and the covered entity does not use the re-identification code or mechanism for any other purposes and does not disclose it.[7]

c. Limited Data Set. Due to concerns that the de-identification standard was so stringent that it might curtail important research, public health, and health care operations activities, DHHS developed the limited data set approach for these purposes.

---

[5] 45 C.F.R. §§ 164.502(d); 164.514(a)–(b).
[6] 45 C.F.R. § 164.514(b).
[7] 45 C.F.R. § 164.514(c).

As with the de-identification safe harbor provisions, the Privacy Regulations specify the direct identifiers that must be removed for a data set to qualify as a limited data set. As with de-identified information, the direct identifiers listed apply to PHI about the individual or about relatives, employers, or household members of the individual. The direct identifiers that must be excluded for a limited data set are:

- Name;
- Street address—Postal address information, other than town/city, state, and zip code;
- Telephone numbers;
- Fax numbers;
- E-mail addresses;
- Social security numbers;
- Medical record numbers;
- Health plan beneficiary numbers;
- Account numbers;
- Certificate/license numbers;
- Vehicle identifiers and serial numbers, including license plate numbers;
- Device identifiers and serial numbers;
- Web addresses—Universal Resource Locators (URLs);
- Internet Protocol (IP) address numbers;
- Biometric identifiers, including fingerprints and voiceprints; and
- Full face photographic images and any other comparable images.[8]

Unlike the list for de-identified information, the list of data elements to be excluded from the limited data set is an exhaustive list. Moreover, in contrast to de-identified data, the limited data set may retain more detailed geographic information (down to the county, city/town, or precinct level and five-digit zip codes) and dates (such as dates of admission and discharge, and dates of birth and death for the individual).[9]

A covered entity may use or disclose a limited data set only for the purposes of research, public health, and health care operations, and only if the covered entity obtains satisfactory assurances, in the form of a data use agreement, that the recipient will only use or disclose the limited data set for limited purposes.[10] The data use agreement between the covered entity and the limited data set recipient must do the following.

- Establish the permitted uses and disclosures of such information by the recipient, which must be for purposes of research, public health, or health care operations. The data use agreement may not authorize the recipient to use or further disclose the information in a manner that would violate the requirements of the Privacy Regulations, if done by the covered entity.
- Establish who is permitted to use or receive the limited data set; and
- Provide that the recipient will:
    - Not use or further disclose the information other than as permitted by the data use agreement or as otherwise required by law;
    - Use appropriate safeguards to prevent use or disclosure of the information other than as provided for by the data use agreement;
    - Report to the covered entity any use or disclosure of the information not provided for by its data use agreement of which it becomes aware;
    - Ensure that any agents, including a subcontractor, to whom it provides the limited data set agrees to the same restrictions and conditions that apply to the limited data set recipient with respect to such information; and
    - Not identify the information or contact the individuals.[11]

---

[8] 45 C.F.R. § 164.514(e)(2).
[9] 67 Fed. Reg. 53235.
[10] 45 C.F.R. § 164.514(e)(3)–(e)(4).
[11] 45 C.F.R. § 164.514(e)(4).

A covered entity is not in compliance with the limited data set standards if the covered entity knew of a pattern of activity or practice of the limited data set recipient that constituted a material breach or violation of the data use agreement, unless the covered entity took reasonable steps to cure the breach or end the violation, as applicable, and, if such steps were unsuccessful, discontinued disclosure of PHI to the recipient, and reported the problem to DHHS.

3. Preemption

In general, the Privacy Regulations will not preempt or be preempted by most other federal or state laws regarding privacy. Covered entities will need to comply with a combination of the Privacy Regulations and other relevant state and federal law, including statutes, regulations, and case law. The required preemption analysis is complex and legal counsel should be consulted; only a summary of this process is included here.

In most cases, state law will be preempted by the Privacy Regulations only if: (i) the state law is "contrary to" HIPAA; i.e., it's impossible to comply with both or the state law creates an obstacle to the accomplishment of the full purposes of the Privacy Regulations; and (ii) the state law relates to individually identifiable health information and is less stringent than the Privacy Regulations.[12] In comparing state law to the Privacy Regulations, the state law will normally be considered more stringent if it prohibits or restricts a use or disclosure that would be permitted under the Privacy Regulations, permits greater rights of access or amendment to the individual, provides more information to the individual (as in a notice of privacy practices), narrows the scope or duration or otherwise increases the privacy protections of an authorization, requires record keeping in more detail or for longer duration, or in general, provides more privacy protections for the individual.[13]

For example, some states have laws providing special protections for mental health records. If these are more stringent than the Privacy Regulations, then the state law is not preempted, and covered entities must comply with both. A careful analysis of state laws regarding privacy will be required to determine the applicable laws after the Privacy Regulations compliance date.

Other federal laws regarding privacy of health information will generally still apply. Conflicting statutes will be interpreted, where possible, to give effect to both. There should be few instances where there is such a conflict under federal law. However, a covered entity will need to review other applicable federal laws to determine what impact HIPAA will have on compliance. Some of these federal laws include the following.

- Medicare conditions of participation applicable to certain health care providers[14]
- Federal substance abuse treatment confidentiality provisions[15]
- Employee Retirement Security Act of 1974 (ERISA)[16]—ERISA preemption analysis is not expected to be affected by the Privacy Regulations preemption analysis.[17]

---

[12]45 C.F.R. § 160.203. State law may also be saved from preemption if the Secretary of DHHS determines the state law provision is necessary to prevent fraud and abuse related to the provision of or payment for health care; to ensure appropriate regulation of insurance and health plans; for state reporting on health care delivery costs; for purposes related to a compelling public health and welfare need; or, its principal purpose is the regulation of a controlled substance. *Id.* State laws providing for the reporting of disease, or injury, child abuse, birth, death, or for public health surveillance, investigation or intervention are also not preempted. Finally, state laws requiring health plans to provide information for management or financial audits, program monitoring and evaluation, or license or certification of facilities or individuals are not preempted. *Id.*

[13]45 C.F.R. § 160.202.

[14]*See* www.cms.hhs.gov/cop/1.asp for a list of citations, according to the type of health care organization.

[15]42 U.S.C. § 290dd-2. 42 C.F.R. Pt. 2.

[16]Pub. L. 93-406.

[17]65 Fed. Reg. 82582.

- Family Educational Rights and Privacy Act (FERPA) provisions relating to school health records[18]
- Gramm-Leach-Bliley Act (GLBA),[19] imposing privacy requirements on financial institutions, including health insurance companies
- The Privacy Act of 1974[20] and the Freedom of Information Act,[21] regarding records maintained by federal agencies
- Clinical Laboratory Improvement Amendments[22]
- Food, Drug, and Cosmetic Act[23]

4. Scalability and Flexibility

The Privacy Regulations are written as general standards, which are intended to be scalable and flexible. All covered entities must take appropriate steps to address privacy concerns, but in determining the scope and extent of their compliance activities, businesses should weigh the costs and benefits of alternative approaches and scale their compliance activities to their structure, functions, and capabilities within the requirements of the regulations.[24] Covered entities will have different privacy needs, depending on their size and complexity. DHHS recognizes that some organizations will need to implement more sophisticated policies and procedures than others.[25]

B. Individual Rights

Under the Privacy Regulations, individuals are given certain new rights with respect to their health care information, as discussed below.

1. Notice of Privacy Practices

A covered entity must prepare a notice of its privacy practices, which describes to the individual the uses and disclosures of PHI that may be made by the covered entity, the individual's rights, and covered entity's legal duties with respect to PHI. There are requirements under the Privacy Regulations relating both to the content of the notice of privacy practices and the distribution of the notice. Moreover, direct treatment providers are required to make a good faith effort to obtain a written acknowledgment of the notice from the individual.[26]

a. Content. The notice of privacy practices must be written in plain language and include all of the following required content elements.[27]

(i) Header: The following statement as a header or otherwise prominently displayed: "THIS NOTICE DESCRIBES HOW MEDICAL INFORMATION ABOUT YOU MAY BE USED AND DISCLOSED AND HOW YOU CAN GET ACCESS TO THIS INFORMATION. PLEASE REVIEW IT CAREFULLY."

---

[18] 20 U.S.C. § 1232g.
[19] Pub. L. 106-102.
[20] 5 U.S.C. § 552a.
[21] 5 U.S.C. § 552.
[22] 42 U.S.C. § 263a; 42 C.F.R. Pt. 493.
[23] 21 U.S.C. § 301 *et seq*.
[24] 65 Fed. Reg. 82785.
[25] 65 Fed. Reg. 82785.
[26] 45 C.F.R. § 164.520. *See* Section III.B.1.b(ii).
[27] 45 C.F.R. § 164.520(b).

(ii) Uses and Disclosures: A description of the uses and disclosures the covered entity may make, including:
- A description, including at least one example, of the types of uses and disclosures the covered entity is permitted by the Privacy Regulations to make for treatment, payment, and health care operations.[28] These descriptions must include sufficient detail to put the individual on notice of the permitted disclosures, and must reflect more stringent state law, if applicable. [Note: The examples selected should be illustrative and meaningful for the individual. The notice of privacy practices should make clear that these are examples only and not a complete list; therefore, using a small number of examples is generally advisable.]
- A description of each of the other purposes for which the covered entity is permitted or required by these regulations to use or disclose PHI without the individual's written authorization. [Note: No examples are required here, but the descriptions must include sufficient detail to put the individual on notice of the required and permitted disclosures, and must reflect more stringent state law, if applicable.]
- A statement that other uses and disclosures will be made only with the individual's written authorization and that the individual may revoke such authorization in writing at any time, except to the extent the covered entity has already relied on the authorization.
- If the covered entity intends to engage in any of the following activities, the description of uses and disclosures must include a separate statement, as follows.
  - Appointment reminders and health-related information: Statement that the covered entity may contact the individual to provide appointment reminders or information about treatment alternatives or other heath-related benefits and services that may be of interest to the individual;
  - Fundraising: Statement that the covered entity may contact the individual to raise funds for the covered entity; or
  - Disclosures to Plan Sponsor: Statement that a group health plan, or a health insurance issuer or HMO with respect to a group health plan, may disclose PHI to the sponsor of the plan.

(iii) Individual Rights: A statement of the individual's rights with respect to PHI and a brief description of how the individual may exercise these rights, as follows.
- The right to request restrictions on certain uses and disclosures of PHI, including a statement that the covered entity is not required to agree to a requested restriction.
- The right to receive confidential communications of PHI.
- The right to inspect and copy PHI.
- The right to amend PHI.
- The right to receive an accounting of certain disclosures of PHI.
- The right to obtain a paper copy of the notice of privacy practices from the covered entity upon request (even if the individual agreed to receive the notice electronically).

(iv) Covered Entity's Duties: A description of the covered entity's duties, including:
- A statement that the covered entity is required by law to maintain the privacy of PHI and to provide individuals with notice of its legal duties and privacy practices with respect to PHI.
- A statement that the covered entity is required to abide by the terms of the notice of privacy practices currently in effect.
- A statement that the covered entity reserves the right to change the terms of its notice of privacy practices and to make the new notice provisions effective for all PHI that it maintains. The statement must also describe how it will provide individuals with a revised notice.

---

[28]*See* Section III.C.2 for definitions of the key HIPAA terms treatment, payment, and health care operations.

(v) Complaints: A statement that individuals may complain to the covered entity and to the Secretary of DHHS if they believe their privacy rights have been violated, a brief description of how the individual may file a complaint with the covered entity, and a statement that the individual will not be retaliated against for filing a complaint.
(vi) Contact: The name or title, and telephone number of a person or office to contact for further information.
(vii) Effective Date: The date on which the notice of privacy practices is first in effect, which may not be earlier than the date on which the notice is printed or otherwise published.

DHHS has suggested using a "layered notice"; that is, a short notice of privacy practices summarizing the individual's rights and other information, with reference to an attached longer notice of privacy practices that contains all of the required elements.[29]

b. Distribution. A covered entity must make the notice of privacy practices available to individuals as follows.[30]

(i) Special Rules for Health Plans

Health plans must provide the notice of privacy practices no later than the compliance date to individuals then covered by the plan; thereafter, notices must be provided to new enrollees at the time of enrollment. At least every three years, the health plan must notify enrollees that the notice is available and how to obtain a copy. A new notice must be provided to enrollees within 60 days if there is a material change. A health plan may satisfy the distribution requirement by providing the notice to the name insured under the policy (and need not provide the notice to each covered dependent). The notice-related obligations of a group health plan vary, depending on whether the plan is insured or self-insured, and whether the plan creates or maintains PHI other than summary information and enrollment information. Refer to Section V for additional information on group health plans.

(ii) Special Rules for Direct Treatment Providers[31]

Definition:

A direct treatment relationship means a treatment relationship between an individual and a health care provider in which the provider–patient relationship involves more than the provider delivering care to the individual based on the orders of another health care provider, or the provider typically providing services or products (or reporting the diagnosis or results associated with the health care) directly to another health care provider who is the one with direct contact with the individual.[32]

Delivery of Notice:

Providers in a direct treatment relationship with the individual must provide the notice of privacy practices no later than the date of the first service delivery after the compliance date. (In an emergency treatment situation, the notice must be provided as soon as reasonably practicable after the emergency.)

---

[29] 67 Fed. Reg. 53243.
[30] 45 C.F.R. § 164.520(c). The notice of privacy practices may be provided electronically under certain circumstances, *see* § 164.520(c)(3). Inmates do not have a right to a notice of privacy practices. 45 C.F.R. § 164.520(a)(3).
[31] 45 C.F.R. § 164.520(c)(2).
[32] 45 C.F.R. § 164.501.

Written Acknowledgment:

A direct treatment provider must make a good faith effort to obtain a written acknowledgement of receipt of the notice of privacy practices from the individual, and if not obtained, document the provider's good faith efforts to obtain such acknowledgment and the reason the acknowledgement was not obtained. In an emergency treatment situation, no acknowledgment is required.[33] The Privacy Regulations do not prescribe the form of the acknowledgement or the process for obtaining it. The individual's signature on the notice of privacy practices is not required; the provider could, instead, have the individual sign or initial a separate form or log sheet.[34] Or, a provider that chooses to obtain a consent from the individual, could design a form that combines the consent and the acknowledgement.[35]

If the first service delivery is over the telephone, the provider may satisfy the notice and acknowledgment requirements by mailing the notice of privacy practices and acknowledgement form to the individual that same day, and requesting that the individual sign the acknowledgment and mail it back to the provider. This would constitute the required good faith effort, even if the individual did not sign and return the acknowledgment form.[36] If the provider's first contact with the individual is just to schedule an appointment, the notice and acknowledgment can wait until the individual arrives for that appointment.[37]

Posting of Notice:

If there is a physical service delivery site, the provider must post the notice of privacy practices at the site in a clear and prominent location, and have copies available for individuals to request and take with them.

Whenever the notice of privacy practices is revised, the provider must make the new notice available on request on or after the effective date of the revision, and if there is a physical delivery site, promptly post the revised notice and make copies available for individuals to request and take with them.

(iii) Notices Upon Request

A covered entity's notice of privacy practices must also be available upon request (by anyone) as of the compliance date.[38]

Making the notice of privacy practices available on request, posting it at a facility or on a Web site, or placing copies on display does not substitute for physically providing the notice directly to the individual.[39]

c. Revisions. The notice of privacy practices must be promptly revised and distributed whenever there is a material change to the covered entity's uses or disclosures, the individual's rights, the covered entity's legal duties, or other privacy practices stated in the notice. Direct treatment providers must make the revised notice available upon request on or after the effective date of the revision, and if there is a physical delivery site, post the revised notice in a clear and prominent location.[40] Except when required by law, a material change to any term of the notice may not be implemented prior to the effective date of the notice in which such material change is reflected. The revision can only apply to PHI received or created by the covered entity after the revised notice is issued, unless the original notice includes the reser-

---

[33] 45 C.F.R. § 164.520(c)(2)(ii).
[34] 67 Fed. Reg. 53240.
[35] 67 Fed. Reg. 53240.
[36] 67 Fed. Reg. 83240.
[37] 67 Fed. Reg. 83240–83241.
[38] 45 C.F.R. § 164.520(c).
[39] 67 Fed. Reg. 53243.
[40] 67 Fed. Reg. 53241.

vation of rights described in paragraph (a)(iv) above.[41] It is not necessary to obtain a new acknowledgment if the notice is revised.[42]

d. Other Notice Issues. All uses and disclosures of PHI by the covered entity, including those related to treatment, payment, and health care operations, must be consistent with the covered entity's notice of privacy practices.[43]

The notice of privacy practices may be used to inform individuals of certain requirements. For example, if the covered entity requires certain requests from individuals, e.g., requests for access or amendments, be in writing, this should be stated in the notice.

The Privacy Regulations contain no specific requirement to translate the notice of privacy practices into other languages. However, Title VI of the Civil Rights Act of 1964 may require the covered entity to provide materials in the primary language of persons with limited English proficiency within the service area.[44]

A covered entity must document compliance with the notice of privacy practices requirements, and retain copies of each version of the notice for six years following the date it is last in effect. Written acknowledgment of receipt of the notice (or documentation of good faith efforts to obtain such acknowledgment), when required, must be retained for six years.[45]

2. Access

An individual has a right to access, inspect, and obtain a copy of his or her PHI.[46] This does not include access to all PHI but only information held by the covered entity in a "designated record set." A designated record set comprises those records used to make decisions about the individual.[47] For providers, this includes medical records and billing records. For health plans, this includes enrollment, payment, claims adjudication, and case or medical management records. A covered entity is not required to provide access to other information that duplicates PHI in the designated record set.[48]

The covered entity may require that the request for access be submitted in writing, if it informs individuals in advance. (This requirement of a written request would be appropriate to include in the notice of privacy practices.) A covered entity must act on a request within 30 days (60 days if the information requested is not on site). This time limit may be extended for another 30 days with written notice to the individual.[49] If the covered entity does not maintain the information requested, but knows where it is maintained, the covered entity must inform the individual where to direct the request for access.[50] The information must be produced in the form or format requested by the individual, if readily producible in that form or format. It may be provided in summary form, if the individual agrees.[51] The covered entity may charge a reasonable cost-based fee for copies, summaries, explanations, and postage.[52]

There are both unreviewable and reviewable grounds for denial of access.[53] The covered entity may deny access, without appeal, for the following types of information.

---

[41] 45 C.F.R. § 164.520(b)(3).
[42] 67 Fed, Reg. 53241.
[43] *See* 67 Fed. Reg. 53211.
[44] 65 Fed. Reg. 82549.
[45] 45 C.F.R. § 164.520(e).
[46] 45 C.F.R. § 164.524.
[47] 45 C.F.R. § 164.501.
[48] 45 C.F.R. § 164.524(c)(1).
[49] 45 C.F.R. § 164.524(b).
[50] 45 C.F.R. § 164.524(d)(3).
[51] 45 C.F.R. § 164.524(c)(2).
[52] 45 C.F.R. § 164.524(c)(4).
[53] 45 C.F.R. § 164.524(a).

- Psychotherapy notes (but not other mental health records)[54]
- Information compiled in reasonable anticipation of a lawsuit
- Information, the release of which is prohibited by CLIA
- Information held by prisons on inmates, based on an assessment of the risks of providing access
- Information held by a research entity, when the individual has agreed to a temporary limitation on access
- Information for which access would be denied under the Privacy Act of 1974
- Information obtained from someone other than a health care provider under a promise of confidentiality, where access would likely reveal the source

The covered entity may deny access, subject to appeal, if the request is for information that the covered entity believes to be reasonably likely to endanger the life or physical safety of the individual or another person, or to cause substantial harm to another person (or to cause substantial harm to the individual, if the request comes from a personal representative). These denials are subject to review by a licensed health professional who did not participate in the original decision to deny access.

A denial of access must be timely and in writing. The denial must explain the basis for the denial, an explanation of the individual's appeal rights, if applicable, a description of the complaint process, and contact information. The covered entity must, to the extent possible, provide the individual with access to other PHI requested.[55]

The covered entity is also required to document the designated record sets that are subject to access by the individual, as well as the titles or offices of those responsible for receiving and processing requests for access.[56] The Privacy Regulations do not specify where this information should be documented. It could be documented in the notice of privacy practices, but if the information changes, the notice would have to be revised. Alternatively, if the covered entity requires these requests in writing, the information could be documented on the form to be used for such requests.

3. Amendments

An individual has the right to have the covered entity amend PHI held by the covered entity in a designated record set.[57] The intent is to ensure that such information is accurate and complete. Amending the record need not mean altering existing information; a covered entity may instead append the amendment to the record or otherwise link the original and amended information.[58] This approach retains the integrity of the original medical record.

The covered entity may require that the request be submitted in writing with an explanation supporting the request, if it so informs the individual.[59] (This requirement of a written request would be appropriate to include in the notice of privacy practices.) The covered entity must act on the request within 60 days. This time limit may be extended for another 30 days with written notice to the individual.[60]

The covered entity may deny the request under certain circumstances, such as if the covered entity did not create the PHI in question, or if the covered entity determines that the

---

[54] See Section III.D for a definition and discussion of psychotherapy notes.
[55] 45 C.F.R. § 164.524(d).
[56] 45 C.F.R. § 164.524(e).
[57] 45 C.F.R. § 164.526.
[58] 45 C.F.R. § 164.526(c)(1).
[59] 45 C.F.R. § 164.526(b)(1).
[60] 45 C.F.R. § 164.526(b)(2).

current information in the record is accurate and complete.[61] The denial must be in writing and must include the following:

- The basis for the denial;
- A statement of the individual's right to submit a statement of disagreement for the record and the process for doing so (such statement of disagreement must be included in future disclosures of the relevant PHI);
- A statement that if a statement of disagreement is not submitted, the individual may ask that the covered entity provide the request for and denial of the amendment with any future disclosures of the relevant PHI; and
- A description of the complaint process and contact information.

The covered entity may prepare a rebuttal to the individual's statement of disagreement. The request for amendment, statement of disagreement, and rebuttal all become part of the designated record set and must be included in future disclosures.[62]

If an amendment is accepted, the covered entity must amend all affected records. In addition, the covered entity must make a reasonable effort to inform persons identified by the individual as having received the information that is to be amended and other persons the covered entity knows have the information and may rely on it (e.g., business associates of the covered entity).[63] Similarly, if the covered entity receives a notice of amendment from another covered entity, it is required to make the appropriate correction/amendment in its records.[64]

As with requests for access, the covered entity is required to document the designated record sets that are subject to amendment requests by the individual, as well as the titles or offices of those responsible for receiving and processing requests for amendments.[65]

4. Accounting of Disclosures

An individual has the right to receive an accounting of disclosures of his or her PHI made by the covered entity in the past six years (although not prior to the compliance date).[66] This accounting of disclosures includes disclosures to or by the business associates of the covered entity.[67] Furthermore, a tracking mechanism will be required for all disclosures subject to this accounting requirement.

This requirement is not applicable to disclosures for treatment, payment, health care operations,[68] disclosures to the individual or his or her personal representative, disclosures made pursuant to an authorization, incidental disclosures, or disclosures for a facility directory or to family/caregivers. Nor is this requirement applicable to disclosures for national security or intelligence purposes, disclosures to law enforcement officials or correctional facilities, or disclosures as part of a limited data set. In addition, under certain circumstances, the covered entity may temporarily suspend an individual's right to information about disclosures to a health oversight or law enforcement official.[69] Thus, the remaining types of disclosures that *will* be subject to this accounting requirement will be primarily disclosures made pursuant to

---

[61] 45 C.F.R. § 164.526(a)(2).
[62] 45 C.F.R. § 164.526(d).
[63] 45 C.F.R. § 164.526(c)(2) - (3).
[64] 45 C.F.R. § 164.526(e).
[65] 45 C.F.R. § 164.526(f).
[66] 45 C.F.R. § 164.528.
[67] 45 C.F.R. § 164.528(b)(1).
[68] *See* Section III.C.2 for definitions of the key HIPAA terms treatment, payment, and health care operations.
[69] 45 C.F.R. § 164.528(a).

45 C.F.R. § 164.512 (other than those specifically included above), disclosures to the Secretary of DHHS, and disclosures mistakenly made contrary to the rules.

The accounting must be in writing and include the date of disclosure, name of recipient (and address, if known), a brief description of the PHI disclosed, and either a statement of the purpose of the disclosure (so as to reasonably inform the individual of the basis for the disclosure) or a copy of a written request for the disclosure (if any). Certain multiple disclosures may be summarized.[70] Special rules apply to accountings related to disclosures for research involving 50 or more individuals, where PHI of the individual requesting the accounting may have been included in a disclosure.[71]

The covered entity must act on the request within 60 days. This time limit may be extended for another 30 days with written notice to the individual.[72] The covered entity must provide the first accounting in any 12-month period without charge, but may charge a reasonable cost-based fee for additional accountings, provided the individual is informed of the costs and given an opportunity to modify the request to avoid or reduce the fee.[73] The Privacy Regulations do not specifically authorize the covered entity to require that a request for an accounting be in writing, but such a requirement is not prohibited.

The covered entity must document the information required to be included in an accounting, the written accountings provided to individuals, and the titles or offices of those responsible for receiving and processing requests for accounting from individuals.[74]

5. Restrictions and Confidential Communications

a. Restrictions. An individual has the right to request restrictions to the covered entity's uses and disclosures of the individual's PHI. The covered entity may deny such a request, but if it grants the request, it is bound by any restriction to which it agrees (except in cases of emergency treatment), and these restrictions must be documented.[75]

b. Confidential Communications. Requests for confidential communications impact providers and health plans differently. A provider must accommodate reasonable requests by individuals to receive PHI communications from the provider at an alternative location or by alternative means. The provider may not require an explanation from the individual as to the basis of the request as a condition for complying, but may require the request be in writing.

A health plan must accommodate reasonable requests by individuals to receive PHI communications from the Plan at alternative locations or by alternative means, if the individual clearly states that the disclosure of all or part of that information could endanger the individual. The Plan may require a statement regarding endangerment as part of a written request for such alternative communications.[76] Such endangerment, for example, could include an individual whose spouse will become physically abusive if he or she discovers the individual has sought treatment. The individual may request, for example, that explanations of benefits and other claim correspondence be mailed to his or her work address rather than his or her home address.

6. No Private Right of Action

There is no private right of action under the Privacy Regulations. That is, the HIPAA statute did not provide for the individual's right to sue for breach of privacy under the regulations.[77]

---

[70] 45 C.F.R. § 164.528(b).
[71] 45 C.F.R. § 164.528(b)(4).
[72] 45 C.F.R. § 164.528(c).
[73] 45 C.F.R. § 164.528(c)(2).
[74] 45 C.F.R. § 164.528(d).
[75] 45 C.F.R. § 164.522(a).
[76] 45 C.F.R. § 164.522(b).
[77] 65 Fed. Reg. 82566.

Nevertheless, in tort or other causes of actions under state law, plaintiffs may argue that the Privacy Regulations establish a standard of care relative to confidentiality of patient information. It is not yet clear how courts will respond to such arguments. However, despite the fact that compliance with the Privacy Regulations was not yet required, one federal court has used the Privacy Regulations' standards as the basis for a decision about the disclosure of medical records.[78]

C. Use and Disclosure of PHI

The main principle of the Privacy Regulations is that PHI may be used or disclosed only as required or permitted under the regulations.[79] The term "use" refers to the sharing, employment, application, utilization, examination, or analysis of PHI within the covered entity that maintains it. The term "disclosure" refers to any release, transfer, provision of access to, or divulging of PHI outside the covered entity maintaining it.[80]

1. Required and Permitted Uses and Disclosures

The Privacy Regulations both require and permit uses and disclosures. Only two types of disclosures are required: (i) to the individual, in accordance with a request for access or request for an accounting of disclosures, as described in Sections III.B.2 and III.B.4; and (ii) to DHHS to investigate a covered entity's compliance with this regulation.

The permitted uses and disclosures are more numerous and are categorized according to their purpose, as follows:

- For treatment, payment, or health care operations, which in some cases requires a good faith effort to obtain the individual's written acknowledgement of receipt of the covered entity's notice of privacy practices;
- For facility directories, provided the individual has been given an opportunity to opt out;
- For disclosures to family and other caregivers, provided the individual has been give an opportunity to opt out;
- For public health purposes, law enforcement purposes, and other limited purposes for which permission of the individual is not required; and
- For other purposes, pursuant to an authorization.[81]

Each of these categories applies in specific circumstances and is discussed in greater detail below.

2. Treatment, Payment, and Health Care Operations

a. Treatment, Payment, and Health Care Operations. Treatment, payment, and health care operations are the most common functions of covered entities.

- *Treatment* includes provision, coordination, or management of health care; consultation between health care providers; or referral of a patient.[82]
- *Payment* includes activities engaged in by a health plan to obtain premiums or to determine or fulfill its responsibilities to provide coverage or benefits; a health plan or pro-

---

[78] United States v. Sutherland, 143 F. Supp. 2d 609, 612 (W.D.Va. 2001) (The Privacy Regulations "indicate a strong federal policy to protect the privacy of patient medical records, and they provide guidance to the present case.").
[79] 45 C.F.R. § 164.502(a).
[80] 45 C.F.R. § 164.501.
[81] 45 C.F.R. § 164.502(a)(1).
[82] 45 C.F.R. § 164.501.

vider providing or obtaining reimbursement for the provision of health care; determinations of eligibility or coverage; coordination of benefits; adjudication or subrogation of health care claims; billing; claims management; utilization review; collection activity; obtaining payment under a reinsurance contract; review of health care services for coverage or medical necessity.[83]

- *Health Care Operations* means the following activities to the extent they are related to the covered functions of the covered entity: Conducting quality assessment or improvement activities; reviewing the competence or qualifications of health care professionals; evaluating health plan performance; conducting health care practitioner and other training programs; accreditation, certification, licensing, or credentialing activities; underwriting, premium rating; medical review; legal services; auditing functions, including fraud and abuse detection and compliance programs; business planning and development; business management; and general administrative activities of the entity.[84] Health care operations also includes a sale, transfer, merger, or consolidation of a covered entity with another covered entity and related transfers of records and due diligence.[85]

b. Consent. Consent to use or disclose PHI for treatment, payment, and health care operations is permitted but not required under the Privacy Regulations.[86] Covered entities that choose to have a consent process have complete discretion in designing that process.[87] Covered entities may, for example, continue to follow consent processes mandated by state law.

c. Acknowledgement of the Notice of Privacy Practices. Obtaining consent to use and disclose PHI for treatment, payment, and health care operations is optional under the Privacy Regulations, which provide "regulatory permission" for these activities.[88] Direct treatment providers are, however, required to take an extra step—to make a good faith effort to obtain a written acknowledgement of receipt of the notice of privacy practices from the individual on the first date of service following the compliance date of the Privacy Regulations. The purpose of the notice of privacy practices and this acknowledgment is to provide individuals with the opportunity to discuss privacy practices and concerns with providers.[89] This acknowledgement is not required for health plans, clearinghouses, indirect treatment providers,[90] or if the individual is an inmate. More information regarding the notice of privacy practices and acknowledgement requirements can be found in Section III.B.1.

d. Disclosures for Treatment, Payment, and Health Care Operations of Another Covered Entity. In addition to using and disclosing PHI for its own treatment, payment, and health care operations, a covered entity may, with certain limitations, disclose PHI for the treatment, payment, and certain health care operations purposes of another entity.[91]

(i) A covered entity may disclose PHI for the <u>treatment</u> activities of any health care provider.

---

[83] 45 C.F.R. § 164.501.

[84] 45 C.F.R. § 164.501. Additional details regarding what constitutes health care operations are found in the regulation and should be referenced before making a final determination as to whether an activity falls into this category.

[85] 45 C.F.R. § 164.501, as modified by 67 Fed. Reg. 53190 (Aug. 14, 2002).

[86] 45 C.F.R. § 164.506(b). Consent may not be obtained in lieu of an authorization, if an authorization is otherwise required under the Privacy Regulations. *Id.* Elimination of the consent requirement was a major change in the Privacy Regulations and was implemented in the modified version of the regulations published August 14, 2002, at 67 Fed. Reg. 53182.

[87] 67 Fed. Reg. 53211.

[88] 67 Fed. Reg. 53211.

[89] 67 Fed. Reg. 53211.

[90] Indirect treatment providers are providers that have only an indirect treatment relationship with the patient, e.g., a clinical laboratory or radiologist that interacts with the referring provider but not the patient. 45 C.F.R. § 164.501.

[91] 45 C.F.R. § 164.506(c).

(ii) A covered entity may disclose PHI to another covered entity or to any health care provider for the <u>payment</u> activities of that recipient.

(iii) A covered entity may disclose PHI to another covered entity for the <u>health care operations</u> of that other entity, if that entity either has or had a relationship with the individual who is the subject of the information,[92] the PHI disclosed pertains to such relationship, and the disclosure is for:
- Conducting quality assessment and improvement activities (including outcomes evaluation and development of clinical guidelines, provided that obtaining generalized knowledge is not the primary purpose of any resulting studies); population-based activities relating to improving health or reducing health care costs; protocol development; case management and care coordination; contacting health care providers and patients with information about treatment alternatives; and related functions that do not include treatment;
- Reviewing the competence or qualifications of health care professionals; evaluating practitioner and provider performance; health plan performance; conducting training programs in which students, trainees, or practitioners in areas of health care learn under supervision to practice or improve their skills as health care providers; training of non-health care professionals; accreditation, certification, licensing, or credentialing activities; or
- The purpose of health care fraud and abuse detection or compliance.

A covered entity that participates in an organized health care arrangement may disclose PHI about an individual to another covered entity that participates in the organized health care arrangement for any health care operations activities of the organized health care arrangement.[93] For example, an HMO may disclose PHI to a group health plan, or a third-party administrator that is a business associate of the group health plan, because the relationship between the HMO and the group health plan is within the definition of an organized health care arrangement for purposes of the Privacy Regulations.[94]

If the Privacy Regulations permit a covered entity to share PHI with another covered entity, the covered entity is permitted to disclose PHI directly to a business associate acting on behalf of that other covered entity. This is true with respect to all of the Privacy Regulations' provisions.[95]

3. Opt Out Approach

The individual's written permission is not required for uses and disclosures for the purposes described in this section, provided the covered entity informs the individual in advance, and the individual has opportunity to object to or restrict these uses or disclosures.[96] Advising the individual of this right and the individual's response may be oral rather than in writing.

---

[92] A covered entity, prior to making a disclosure allowed under this requirement, is permitted to communicate with another covered entity as necessary to determine if this condition has been met. 67 Fed. Reg. 53217. Where the relationship between the covered entity and the individual has ended, a disclosure of PHI about the individual is permitted to the extent the disclosure is related to the past relationship. For example, a health care provider may disclose PHI to a health plan for HEDIS purposes, even if the individual no longer was covered by the health plan, provided that the period for which information is needed overlaps with period for which the individual was enrolled in the health plan. *Id.* For disclosures of PHI for quality and other health care operations where the covered entity requesting the information does not have a relationship with the individual, the provisions for limited data sets are intended to provide a mechanism for disclosures of PHI. *Id. See* Section III.A.2 for a discussion of limited data sets.
[93] 45 C.F.R. § 164.506(c)(5).
[94] 67 Fed. Reg. 53218.
[95] 67 Fed. Reg. 53218.
[96] 45 C.F.R. § 164.510.

a. Facility Directory.[97] Under certain circumstances, a provider with a facility directory may include in that directory, the individual's:

- Name;
- Location in the facility;
- General condition in terms that do not communicate specific medical information about the individual (e.g., fair, critical, stable, etc.); and
- Religious affiliation.

The above may be included in the directory if the individual does not object to being included in the directory; and if the provider informs individuals in advance what PHI may be included in the facility directory and to whom disclosures may be made, and gives the individual a meaningful opportunity to opt out of the directory listing or to restrict some or all of the uses and disclosures in regard to the directory (e.g., omitting religious affiliation or general condition from the directory information). Subject to the individual's right to object, the provider may disclose the directory information (except religious affiliation) to anyone who asks for the individual by name. All directory information, including religious affiliation, may be disclosed to members of the clergy, and they need not ask for the individual by name.

The Privacy Regulations allow such directory-type disclosures when individuals are incapacitated and in emergency treatment circumstances; in such situations, the provider must make the decision whether to include the individual's information in the facility directory in accordance with professional judgment as to the individual's best interest. The provider must, when it becomes practicable, inform the individual about its policies regarding the facility directory and provide the opportunity to object to the use or disclosure of PHI for the directory.

b. Current Caregivers.[98] Covered entities may disclose to a person involved in the current health care of the individual (such as a family member, other relative, close personal friend, or any other person identified by the individual) PHI directly related to the person's involvement in the current health care of the individual or payment related to that health care. Covered entities may also use or disclose PHI to notify or assist in notification of family members, personal representatives, or other persons responsible for an individual's care with respect to an individual's location, condition, or death.

When the individual is present at the time of disclosure and has the capacity to make his or her own decisions, a covered entity may use or disclose PHI only if it: (i) obtains the individual's agreement to disclose to the third parties involved in their care; (ii) provides the individual with an opportunity to object to such disclosure and the individual does not express an objection; or (iii) reasonably infers from the circumstances, based on the exercise of professional judgment, that the individual does not object to the disclosure. Situations in which providers may infer an individual's agreement to disclose PHI include, for example, when a patient brings a spouse into the doctor's office when treatment is being discussed, or when a friend has brought the individual to the emergency room for treatment.

When the individual is not present or when the opportunity to agree or object to the use or disclosure cannot practicably be provided due to the individual's incapacity or an emergency circumstance, covered entities may, in the exercise of professional judgment, determine whether the disclosure is in the individual's best interests and if so, disclose only the PHI that is directly relevant to the person's involvement with the individual's health care. For example, this provision allows covered entities to inform relatives or others involved in a patient's care, such as the person who accompanied the patient to the emergency room, that a patient has

---

[97] 45 C.F.R. § 164.510(a); 65 Fed. Reg. 82521.
[98] 45 C.F.R. § 164.510(b); 65 Fed. Reg. 82522.

suffered a heart attack and to provide updates on the patient's progress and prognosis when the patient is incapacitated and unable to make decisions about such disclosures. The Privacy Regulations are not intended to disrupt most current practices with respect to these types of disclosures.

A covered entity may also use or disclose PHI to a public or private disaster relief organization in order for that organization to locate a family member or other individual involved in the individual's care.

4. Uses and Disclosures for Which No Permission Is Required

DHHS recognized that certain uses and disclosures of PHI are essential for public health, law enforcement, and the operation of the health care system. To require the individual's permission for these uses and disclosures would present an unacceptable obstacle to these public purposes. Therefore, uses and disclosures for the following purposes do not require the individual's permission or an opportunity to opt out.[99]

a. Uses and Disclosures Required by Law. Covered entities may use and disclose PHI where required by law, provided the use or disclosure complies with and is limited to the relevant requirements of that law. Additional requirements apply if the purpose of the disclosures relates to victims of abuse, neglect, or domestic violence; disclosures for judicial or administrative proceedings; or disclosures for law enforcement.[100]

b. Public Health Activities[101]. Covered entities may disclose PHI for the following public purposes to the following entities.

(i) Public Health Reporting. A covered entity may disclose PHI to a public health authority authorized by law to collect or receive such information for the purpose of preventing or controlling disease, injury, or disability. Examples include the reporting of disease, injury, vital events (such as birth or death), and the conduct of public health surveillance, public health investigations, and public health interventions; or, at the direction of a public health authority, to an official of a foreign government agency that is acting in collaboration with a public health authority.

(ii) Child Abuse or Neglect. A covered entity may disclose PHI to a public health authority or other appropriate government authority authorized by law to receive reports of child abuse or neglect.

(iii) Food and Drug Administration (FDA) Regulation. A covered entity may disclose PHI to a person subject to the jurisdiction of the FDA with respect to an FDA-regulated product or activity for which that person has responsibility, for the purpose of activities related to the quality, safety, or effectiveness of such FDA-regulated product or activity. Such purposes include, but are not limited to, the following activities and purposes: (A) to collect or report adverse events (or similar activities regarding food or dietary supplements), product defects or problems (including problems with the use or labeling of a product), or biological product deviations; (B) to track FDA-regulated products; (C) to enable product recalls, repairs, or replacement, or for lookback (including locating and notifying persons who have received products that have been withdrawn, recalled, or are the subject of lookback); and (D) to conduct post-marketing surveillance.

(iv) Communicable Disease. A covered entity may disclose PHI to a person who may have been exposed to a communicable disease or may otherwise be at risk of contracting or spreading a disease or condition, if the covered entity or public health authority is

---

[99] 45 C.F.R. § 164.512.
[100] 45 C.F.R. § 164.512(a), *referencing* 45 C.F.R. § 164.512(c), (e), and (f).
[101] 45 C.F.R. § 164.512(b).

authorized by law to notify such person as necessary in the conduct of a public health intervention or investigation.

(v) <u>Employers</u>. A covered entity may disclose PHI to an employer, about an individual who is a member of the workforce of the employer, if four requirements are met: (A) the covered entity is a provider who is a member of the workforce of the employer or who provides health care to the individual at the request of the employer, to conduct an evaluation relating to medical surveillance of the workplace; or to evaluate whether the individual has a work-related illness or injury; (B) the PHI that is disclosed consists of findings concerning a work-related illness or injury or a workplace-related medical surveillance; (C) the employer needs such findings in order to comply with its obligations, under the Occupational Safety and Health Hazards Act (OSHA), or other federal or state law regarding workplace illness or injury, or to carry out responsibilities for workplace medical surveillance; and (D) the provider gives written notice to the individual that PHI relating to the medical surveillance of the workplace and work-related illnesses and injuries is disclosed to the employer, either by giving a copy of the notice to the individual at the time the health care is provided; or, if the health care is provided on the work site of the employer, by posting the notice in a prominent place at the location where the health care is provided.

If the covered entity also is a public health authority, the covered entity is permitted to use PHI in all cases in which it is permitted to disclose such information for public health activities, as described above.

c. Victims of Abuse, Neglect, or Domestic Violence.[102] A covered entity may disclose PHI about an individual whom it reasonably believes to be a victim of abuse, neglect, or domestic violence to a government authority, including a social service or protective services agency, authorized by law to receive reports of such abuse, neglect, or domestic violence, under the following circumstances:

- The disclosure is required by law and complies with and is limited to the relevant requirements of such law;
- If the individual agrees to the disclosure; or
- The disclosure is expressly authorized by statute or regulation and, (A) the covered entity, in the exercise of professional judgment, believes the disclosure is necessary to prevent serious harm to the individual or other potential victims; or (B) if the individual is unable to agree because of incapacity, a law enforcement or other public official authorized to receive the report represents that the PHI for which disclosure is sought is not intended to be used against the individual and that an immediate enforcement activity that depends upon the disclosure would be materially and adversely affected by waiting until the individual is able to agree to the disclosure.

Reports of child abuse or neglect should, however, be handled in accordance with Section III.C.4(b)(ii).

The covered entity must promptly inform the individual that such a report has been or will be made, except if the covered entity, in the exercise of professional judgment, believes that informing the individual would place the individual at risk of serious harm; or if the covered entity would be informing a personal representative, and the covered entity reasonably believes the personal representative is responsible for the abuse, neglect, or other injury, and in the professional judgment of the covered entity, informing such person would not be in the best interests of the individual.

---

[102] 45 C.F.R. § 164.512(c).

d. Health Oversight Activities[103]. A covered entity may disclose PHI to a health oversight agency for oversight activities authorized by law, including audits; civil, administrative, or criminal investigations; inspections; licensure or disciplinary actions; or, civil, administrative, or criminal proceedings or actions. Disclosure is also permitted for other activities necessary for appropriate oversight of the health care system; government benefit programs (for which health information is relevant to beneficiary eligibility); entities subject to government regulatory programs (for which health information is necessary for determining compliance with program standards); or, entities subject to civil rights laws for which health information is necessary for determining compliance.

Such health oversight activity does not include an investigation or other activity in which the individual is the subject of the investigation or activity and such investigation or other activity does not arise out of and is not directly related to one of the following: the receipt of health care; a claim for public benefits related to health; or qualification for, or receipt of, public benefits or services when a patient's health is integral to the claim for public benefits or services.

If a covered entity also is a health oversight agency, it may use PHI for health oversight activities for which disclosure is permitted, as described above.

e. Judicial and Administrative Proceedings. A covered entity may disclose PHI in the course of any judicial or administrative proceeding, which is:

- In response to an order of a court or administrative tribunal (but only to the extent expressly authorized by such order); or
- In response to a subpoena, discovery request, or other lawful process, that is not accompanied by an order of a court or administrative tribunal, if the covered entity receives satisfactory assurance from the party seeking the information that reasonable efforts have been made by such party to ensure that the individual who is the subject of the PHI requested has been given notice of the request; or the covered entity receives satisfactory assurance from the party seeking the information that reasonable efforts have been made by such party to secure a qualified protective order.[104]

f. Law Enforcement. A covered entity may disclose PHI for a law enforcement purpose to a law enforcement official if the following conditions are met, as applicable.

(i) Pursuant to process and as otherwise required by law

A covered entity may disclose PHI as required by law; for example, where state law requires a provider to report certain types of wounds or other physical injuries. (Except, with regard to child abuse or neglect, see Section III.C.4(b)(ii), and with regard to other abuse or neglect or domestic violence, see Section III.C.4(c)). A covered entity may also disclose PHI in accordance with any of the following: a court order or court-ordered warrant, or a subpoena or summons issued by a judicial officer; a grand jury subpoena; or an administrative request, such as an administrative subpoena or summons, a civil or an authorized investigative demand, or similar process authorized under law. The information sought must be relevant and material to a legitimate law enforcement inquiry. The request must be specific and limited in scope; and it must be the case that de-identified information could not reasonably be used.[105]

---

[103] 45 C.F.R. § 164.512(d).
[104] 45 C.F.R. § 164.512(e). Refer to 45 C.F.R. §§ 164.512(e)(1)(iii)–(vi) regarding what will constitute "satisfactory assurances" and the requirements for a qualified protective order.
[105] *See* Section III.A.2 for a discussion of de-identified information.

(ii) Limited information for identification and location purposes

In response to a law enforcement official's request for information for the purpose of identifying or locating a suspect, fugitive, material witness, or missing person, a covered entity may disclose the following limited PHI:

- Name and address;
- Date and place of birth;
- Social Security number;
- ABO blood type and rh factor;
- Type of injury;
- Date and time of treatment;
- Date and time of death (if applicable); and
- Description of distinguishing physical characteristics, including height, weight, gender, race, hair and eye color, presence or absence of facial hair, scars and tattoos.

Disclosure of the individual's DNA or DNA analysis; dental records; or typing, samples or analysis of body fluids or tissue, may not be disclosed for identification or location purposes.

(iii) Victims of a crime

A covered entity may disclose PHI in response to a law enforcement official's request for information about an individual who is, or is suspected to be, a victim of a crime, if the individual agrees to the disclosure. If the covered entity is unable to obtain the individual's agreement because of incapacity or other emergency circumstance, the PHI may be disclosed if the covered entity determines in its professional judgment that such disclosure is in the best interest of the individual, and the law enforcement official represents that such information is needed to determine whether another person has violated the law; such information is not intended to be used against the victim; and immediate law enforcement activity that depends upon the disclosure would be materially and adversely affected by waiting until the individual is able to agree to the disclosure.

(iv) Decedents

A covered entity may disclose PHI about an individual who has died to a law enforcement official for the purpose of alerting law enforcement of the death of the individual if the covered entity suspects that such death may have resulted from criminal conduct.

(v) Crime on premises

A covered entity may disclose to a law enforcement official PHI that the covered entity believes in good faith constitutes evidence of criminal conduct that occurred on the premises of the covered entity.

(vi) Reporting crime in emergencies

A provider providing emergency health care in response to a medical emergency not on its own premises, may disclose PHI to a law enforcement official if such disclosure appears necessary to alert law enforcement to the commission and nature of a crime; the location or victim of such crime; or the identity, description, and location of the perpetrator of such crime.

If the provider believes that the medical emergency is the result of abuse, neglect, or domestic violence of the individual in need of emergency health care, this provision does not apply, and any disclosure to a law enforcement official is subject to Section III.C.4(c).[106]

---

[106] 45 C.F.R. § 164.512(f).

g. Research Purposes. The Privacy Regulations attempt to strike a balance between protecting the privacy of individually identifiable health information, and ensuring that researchers continue to have access to medical information necessary to conduct vital research. Currently, most research involving human subjects operates under the Common Rule (codified for DHHS at Title 45 Code of Federal Regulations Part 46) and/or the FDA human subjects protection regulations. These other federal laws have some provisions that are similar to, but more stringent than and separate from, the Privacy Regulations' provisions regarding research.[107]

Under the Privacy Regulation, a covered entity may always use or disclose de-identified information for research purposes, or a limited data set under a data use agreement.[108] Furthermore, an authorization may be obtained from the individual to use or disclose his or her PHI for research purposes.[109] However, if the covered entity intends to use or disclose PHI without an authorization by the research subject, the following conditions must be met, as applicable.

(i) For research without an authorization, the covered entity provides documentation that an Institutional Review Board (IRB) or a Privacy Board has approved an alteration or waiver of research participants' authorization for use/disclosure of their PHI for research purposes. This provision of the Privacy Regulations might be used, for example, to conduct records research when researchers are unable to use de-identified information and it is not practicable to obtain research participants' authorization.

A valid waiver of authorization from the IRB or Privacy Board requires documentation of all of the following:[110]

- A statement that the alteration or waiver of authorization was approved by an IRB or Privacy Board that was composed as described in the Privacy Regulations;[111]
- A statement identifying the IRB or Privacy Board and the date on which the alteration or waiver of authorization was approved;
- A statement that the IRB or Privacy Board has determined that the alteration or waiver of authorization, in whole or in part, satisfies the following criteria:
  (A) The use or disclosure of PHI involves no more than minimal risk to the privacy of individuals, based on, at least, the presence of the following elements:
    – An adequate plan to protect the identifiers from improper use and disclosure;
    – An adequate plan to destroy the identifiers at the earliest opportunity consistent with conduct of the research, unless there is a health or research justification for retaining the identifiers or such retention is otherwise required by law; and
    – Adequate written assurances that the PHI will not be reused or disclosed to any other person or entity, except as required by law, for authorized oversight of the research study, or for other research for which the use or disclosure of PHI would be permitted by this subpart;
  (B) The research could not practicably be conducted without the waiver or alteration;
  (C) The research could not practicably be conducted without access to and use of the PHI;
- A brief description of the PHI for which use or access has been determined to be necessary by the IRB or Privacy Board;
- A statement that the alteration or waiver of authorization has been reviewed and approved under either normal or expedited review procedures as described in the Privacy Regulations[112]; and

---

[107]DHHS Office of Civil Rights Guidance on the Privacy Regulations, issued July 6, 2001, available at *www.hhs.gov/ocr/hipaa/assist.html* ("July 2001 Guidance").
[108]*See* Section III.A.2 for a discussion of de-identified information and limited data sets.
[109]*See* Section III.C.5 for a discussion of authorizations.
[110]45 C.F.R. § 164.512(i)(1)(i) and 512(i)(2).
[111]45 C.F.R. § 164.512(i)(i)(i).
[112]45 C.F.R. § 164.512(i)(2)(iv)(setting forth references to Common Rule procedures for an IRB, and certain other procedures for Privacy Boards).

- The signature of the chair or other member, as designated by the chair, of the IRB or the Privacy Board, as applicable.

(ii) For reviews preparatory to research, the covered entity obtains representations from the researcher, either in writing or orally, that the use or disclosure of the PHI is solely to prepare a research protocol or for similar purposes preparatory to research, that the researcher will not remove any PHI from the covered entity in the course of the review, *and* that PHI for which access is sought is necessary for the research purpose. This provision might be used, for example, to design a research study or to assess the feasibility of conducting a study.

(iii) For research on decedents, the covered entity obtains representations from the researcher, either in writing or orally, that the use or disclosure being sought is solely for research on the PHI of decedents, that the PHI being sought is necessary for the research, *and*, at the request of the covered entity, documentation of the death of the individuals about whom information is being sought.[113]

h. To Avert a Serious Threat to Health or Safety[114]. A covered entity may, consistent with applicable law and standards of ethical conduct, use or disclose PHI, if it believes in good faith that the use or disclosure: (A) is necessary to prevent or lessen a serious and imminent threat to the health or safety of a person or the public, and disclosure is to a person or persons reasonably able to prevent or lessen the threat, including the target of the threat; or (B) is necessary for law enforcement authorities to identify or apprehend an individual, because of a statement by an individual admitting participation in a violent crime that the covered entity reasonably believes may have caused serious physical harm to the victim; or where it appears from all the circumstances that the individual has escaped from a correctional institution or from lawful custody. A covered entity's good faith is presumed if its beliefs in this regard are based upon actual knowledge or in reliance on a credible representation by a person with apparent knowledge or authority.

In the case of a statement by an individual admitting participation in a violent crime, as described above, certain additional limitations apply. A disclosure made pursuant to such statement may only contain (A) the statement made by the individual, and (B) any of the following limited PHI:

- Name and address;
- Date and place of birth;
- Social security number;
- ABO blood type and rh factor;
- Type of injury;
- Date and time of treatment; and
- Date and time of death (if applicable).

Furthermore, use or disclosure is not permitted if the PHI is learned by the covered entity in the course of treatment to affect the propensity to commit such criminal conduct, or in the course of counseling or therapy (or through a request by the individual to initiate or to be referred for such treatment, counseling, or therapy).

i. Specialized Government Functions. The covered entity may use and disclose PHI in various circumstances involving specialized governmental functions, including military and veterans activities, national security and intelligence activities, protective services for the President and others, medical suitability determinations by the State Department, correctional institutions and other law enforcement custodial situations, and covered entities that are

---

[113] 45 C.F.R. § 164.512(i); July 2001 Guidance.
[114] 45 C.F.R. § 164.512(j).

government programs providing public benefits. The regulatory language should be consulted for additional information in these areas.[115]

j. Workers' Compensation. A covered entity may disclose PHI as authorized by and to the extent necessary to comply with laws relating to workers' compensation or other similar programs, established by law, that provide benefits for work-related injuries or illness without regard to fault.[116]

k. Decedents. Special rules apply to PHI about decedents and cadaveric organ donations. *See* Section III.D.5.

In cases where the covered entity is required to inform the individual of, or where the individual may agree to, a use or disclosure permitted by any of the provisions in this Section III.C.4, these communications may be oral rather than in writing.[117]

5. All Other Purposes—Authorization

a. General Rule. For uses and disclosures that are not otherwise expressly permitted or required, covered entities must obtain the individual's authorization.[118] An authorization gives the covered entity permission to use particular PHI or disclose that PHI to a specified third party for a specified purpose. The covered entity must document and retain such signed authorizations.[119]

Covered entities may use only authorizations that meet the requirements of the Privacy Regulations, and any such use or disclosure will be lawful only to the extent it is consistent with the terms of such authorization. Thus, neither a voluntary consent document nor a written acknowledgement of the notice of privacy practices will constitute a valid permission to use or disclose PHI for a purpose that requires an authorization.[120]

b. Examples of When an Authorization Is Required.

- Use or disclosure of psychotherapy notes, other than by the originator of the notes, with limited exceptions.[121]
- Disclosures of a child's PHI for direct disclosure to the child's school to permit the child's participation in sports activities.
- Sale of a patient list (e.g., an obstetrician's sale of patient names and addresses to a diaper service).
- Disclosure of PHI to an employer for employment decisions.
- Disclosure of PHI to a life insurer for underwriting/eligibility for insurance.
- Fundraising, with limited exceptions.[122]
- Marketing, with exceptions.[123]

Covered entities will need a process for determining whether the appropriate authorization has been obtained, what it specifically permits, and whether it is still valid.

c. Format and Content of an Authorization. An authorization is written in specific and customized terms. Incomplete, revoked, or expired authorizations are not valid.[124]

---

[115] 45 C.F.R. § 164.512(k).
[116] 45 C.F.R. § 164.512(l).
[117] 45 C.F.R. § 164.512.
[118] 45 C.F.R. § 164.508.
[119] 45 C.F.R. § 164.508(b)(6).
[120] 45 C.F.R. § 164.508(a); see 67 Fed. Reg. 53220.
[121] *See* Section III.D.3 for a discussion of psychotherapy notes and mental health records.
[122] *See* Section III.D.1 for a discussion of fundraising.
[123] *See* Section III.D.2 for a discussion of marketing.
[124] 45 C.F.R. § 164.508(b)(2).

(i) A valid authorization must contain the following core elements:[125]

- A description of the information to be used or disclosed that identifies the information in a specific and meaningful fashion;
- The name or other specific identification of the person(s), or class of persons, authorized to make the requested use or disclosure;
- The name or other specific identification of the person(s), or class of persons, to whom the covered entity may make the requested use or disclosure;
- A description of each purpose of the requested use or disclosure (the statement "at the request of the individual" is sufficient, if the individual initiates the authorization and does not provide a statement of the purpose.);
- An expiration date or an expiration event that relates to the individual or the purpose of the use or disclosure (for example, the expiration event might be the initial release of the information, i.e., a one-time release). For research purposes only, including the creation and maintenance of a research database or research repository, the statement "end of the research study" or "none" is sufficient; and
- Signature of the individual and date (If the authorization is signed by a personal representative of the individual, a description of such representative's authority to act for the individual is also required.).

(ii) A valid authorization must also contain all of the following core statements, written in a manner that is adequate to put the individual on notice of the substance of these statements:[126]

- A statement of the individual's right to revoke the authorization in writing and either: (A) the exceptions to the right to revoke, together with a description of how the individual may revoke the authorization; or (B) to the extent this same information is included in the notice of privacy practices, a reference to that notice;
- A statement regarding whether or not treatment, payment, enrollment, or eligibility for benefits may be conditioned on the authorization, by stating either: (A) the covered entity may not condition treatment, payment, enrollment, or eligibility for benefits on whether the individual signs the authorization when the Privacy Regulations prohibit such conditioning of authorizations (*See* Section III.C.5(e)); or (B) the consequences to the individual of a refusal to sign the authorization when, in accordance with the Privacy Regulations, the covered entity can condition treatment, enrollment in the health plan, or eligibility for benefits on failure to obtain such authorization; and
- A statement that information used or disclosed pursuant to the authorization may be subject to redisclosure by the recipient and no longer be protected by the Privacy Regulations (e.g., if the disclosure is to other than a covered entity). A general statement of this possibility is sufficient; no analysis of the risk of redisclosure is required.[127] A covered entity may provide additional information at its discretion; for example, when requesting an authorization for its own uses of PHI, the covered entity may provide assurances that the information will remain subject to the Privacy Regulations.[128]

(iii) A valid authorization must be written in plain language.[129]

---

[125] 45 C.F.R. § 164.508(c)(1).
[126] 45 C.F.R. § 164.508(c)(2).
[127] 67 Fed. Reg. 53221.
[128] 67 Fed. Reg. 53222.
[129] 45 C.F.R. § 164.508(c)(3).

(iv) A valid authorization may contain elements or information in addition to the elements listed above, provided that such additional elements or information are not inconsistent with the required elements.[130]

If the covered entity seeks the authorization from the individual, the individual must be provided with a copy of the signed authorization.[131]

d. Compound Authorizations. An authorization may not be combined with any other document, except as follows.[132]

- An authorization for a research study may be in the same document as any other type of written permission for the same research study, including another authorization for the use or disclosure of PHI for such research or a consent to participate in such research.
- An authorization for a use or disclosure of psychotherapy notes may only be combined with another authorization for a use or disclosure of psychotherapy notes.
- An authorization (other than for psychotherapy notes) may be combined with any other such authorization under this section, except when a covered entity has conditioned the provision of treatment, payment, enrollment in the health plan, or eligibility for benefits on the provision of one of the authorizations.

e. Conditioning of Authorizations. A covered entity may not condition the provision of treatment, payment, enrollment in the health plan, or eligibility for benefits on the provision of an authorization, except as follows.[133]

- A provider may condition the provision of research-related treatment on provision of an authorization for the use or disclosure of PHI for such research.
- A health plan may condition enrollment in the health plan or eligibility for benefits on provision of an authorization requested by the health plan prior to an individual's enrollment in the health plan, if: (A) the authorization sought is for the health plan's eligibility or enrollment determinations relating to the individual or for its underwriting or risk rating determinations; and (B) the authorization is not for a use or disclosure of psychotherapy notes.
- A covered entity may condition the provision of health care that is solely for the purpose of creating PHI for disclosure to a third party on provision of an authorization for the disclosure of the PHI to such third party. For example, a provider may have a contract with an employer to provide fitness-for-duty exams for the employer's employees. The provider may refuse to conduct the exam if the individual refuses to authorize disclosure of the exam results to the employer.[134]

f. Revoking an Authorization. An individual may revoke an authorization at any time, provided that the revocation is in writing, except: (A) to the extent that the covered entity has taken action in reliance on the authorization; or (B) if the authorization was obtained as a condition of obtaining insurance coverage, and other law provides the insurer with the right to contest a claim under the policy or the policy itself.[135]

g. Transition Provisions. If express permission for use or disclosure of PHI is obtained before the compliance date, the covered entity may rely on such permission after the compli-

---

[130] 45 C.F.R. § 164.508(b)(1)(ii).
[131] 45 C.F.R. § 164.508(c)(3).
[132] 45 C.F.R. § 164.508(b)(3).
[133] 45 C.F.R. § 164.508(b)(4).
[134] 65 Fed. Reg. 82516.
[135] 45 C.F.R. § 164.508(b)(5).

ance date (but must abide by its terms). This generally applies only with respect to information created or received prior to the compliance date.[136] Special transition provisions apply to research purposes.[137]

h. Documentation. A covered entity must document and retain any signed authorization under this section for six years from the date of its creation or the date it was last in effect, whichever is later.[138]

D. Special Applications of the Rules Relating to Uses and Disclosures

1. Fundraising

A special fundraising provision[139] permits a covered entity to use or disclose PHI without authorization for fundraising on its own behalf, provided that it limits that PHI to: (i) demographic information about the individual; and (ii) the dates that the covered entity has provided service to the individual. In addition, such fundraising materials must explain how the individual may opt out of any further fundraising communications, and covered entities must make reasonable efforts to honor such requests. Therefore, a process for tracking opt-outs will be required. In addition, the covered entity's notice of privacy practices must contain a statement that the covered entity may contact the individual to raise funds for the covered entity. Fundraising that is not on behalf of the covered entity would require a written authorization from the individual.

A covered entity may disclose this limited PHI (demographics and dates of service) only to a business associate (as defined in Section III.F) or an institutionally related foundation. An "institutionally related foundation" is a foundation that qualifies as a nonprofit charitable foundation under § 501(c)(3) of the Internal Revenue Code and has in its charter statement of charitable purposes an explicit linkage to the covered entity. The term does not include an organization with a general charitable purpose. For example, a covered hospital may disclose, for fundraising on its own behalf, the limited PHI to a nonprofit foundation established for the specific purpose of raising funds for the hospital or to a foundation that has as its mission the support of the members of a particular hospital chain that includes the covered hospital.

2. Marketing

The general rule is that authorization is required for uses and disclosures of PHI for marketing purposes.[140] The definition of "marketing" is quite broad, yet it has so many exceptions that most communications of a health care provider or health plan will not require authorization even though they might seem to be marketing-related activities.

As defined by the Privacy Regulations, "marketing" means:

a. To make a communication about a product or service that encourages recipients of the communication to purchase or use the product or service, <u>unless</u> the communication is made:
   - To describe a health-related product or service (or payment for such product or service) that is provided by, or included in a plan of benefits of, the covered entity making the communication, including communications about: the entities participating in a health care provider network or health plan network; replacement of, or enhancements to, a health plan; and health-related products or services available only to a health plan enrollee that add value to, but are not part of, a plan of benefits;

---

[136] 45 C.F.R. § 164.532.
[137] 45 C.F.R. § 164.532; 67 Fed. Reg. 53248.
[138] 45 C.F.R. § 164.508(b)(6).
[139] 45 C.F.R. § 164.514(f); 65 Fed. Reg. 82546.
[140] 45 C.F.R. § 164.508(a)(3).

- For treatment of the individual; or
- For case management or care coordination for the individual, or to direct or recommend alternative treatments, therapies, health care providers, or settings of care to the individual.

b. An arrangement between a covered entity and any other entity whereby the covered entity discloses PHI to the other entity, in exchange for direct or indirect remuneration, for the other entity or its affiliate to make a communication about its own product or service that encourages recipients of the communication to purchase or use that product or service.[141]

Furthermore, although they may be marketing activities, a covered entity does not need authorization if it uses or discloses PHI for marketing under the following conditions.[142]

a. A covered entity may use or disclose PHI in a marketing communication with the individual in a face-to-face encounter.
b. A covered entity may provide promotional gifts of nominal value (e.g., distributing sample products or pens/calendars with its own or another company's name or product name on them).

This approach accommodates the needs of health care entities to be able to discuss their own health-related products and services, or those of third parties, as part of their everyday business and as part of promoting the health of their patients and enrollees.

If a communication is classified as marketing and involves direct or indirect remuneration to the covered entity from a third party, the authorization must state that such remuneration is involved;[143] for example, a covered entity sells its patient list or receives payment from a third party for PHI that the third party will use in promoting its own products or services.

3. Mental Health Records and Psychotherapy Notes

The Privacy Regulations generally do not treat any category of PHI (e.g., mental health, substance abuse, or AIDS records) as more sensitive than any other, and the protections are generally uniform.[144] There are, however, special rules relating to psychotherapy notes. The term "psychotherapy notes" refers only to the notes recorded (in any medium) by a health care provider who is a mental health professional documenting or analyzing a conversation during an individual, group, or family counseling session. These records, by definition, are kept separate from the rest of the individual's medical record. Psychotherapy notes do not include medication prescription and management, counseling session start and stop times, the modalities and frequencies of treatment, results of clinical tests, or any summary of diagnosis, functional status, treatment plan, symptoms, prognosis, or progress to date.[145]

These private notes of a mental health professional receive additional protection under the Privacy Regulations. In general, covered entities must obtain the individual's authorization in order to use or disclose psychotherapy notes.[146] The following are the only circumstances in which an authorization is not required:

a. To carry out the following treatment, payment, or health care operations:
- Use (but not disclosure) by the originator of the psychotherapy notes for treatment purposes;

---

[141] 45 C.F.R. § 164.501.
[142] 45 C.F.R. § 164.508(a)(3)(i).
[143] 45 C.F.R. § 164.508(a)(3)(ii).
[144] Any state law, however, which provides a higher level of protection to such records will generally still apply, under the preemption analysis discussed in Section III.A.3.
[145] 45 C.F.R. § 164.501.
[146] 45 C.F.R. § 164.508(a)(2).

- Use or disclosure by the covered entity for its own training programs in which students, trainees, or practitioners in mental health learn under supervision to practice or improve their skills in group, joint, family, or individual counseling; or
- Use or disclosure by the covered entity to defend itself in a legal action or other proceeding brought by the individual;

b. For uses and disclosures:
- Required by DHHS to investigate compliance with the Privacy Regulations;
- Required by law;
- To comply with a request from a health care oversight agency with respect to oversight of the originator of the psychotherapy notes;
- To coroners or medical examiners regarding a deceased individual; or,
- To prevent or lessen a serious and imminent threat to the health or safety of a person or the public.

4. Underwriting

PHI may be used or disclosed for underwriting and other activities relating to the creation, renewal, or replacement of a contract of health insurance or health benefits. Health plans receiving PHI for these purposes may not use or disclose it for any other purpose, except as may be required by law, if the insurance or benefits contract is not placed with the health plan. Health plans must develop a process to assure that the PHI is appropriately disposed of if the application for health insurance is unsuccessful.[147]

5. Special Categories of Individuals

a. Personal Representatives. A covered entity must treat a personal representative of an individual as the individual for purposes of the Privacy Regulations, if such person is, under applicable law, authorized to act on behalf of the individual in making decisions related to health care.[148] This includes a court-appointed guardian and a person with a power of attorney, but may also include other persons. This provision applies to persons empowered under state or other law to make health-related decisions for an individual, whether or not the instrument or law granting such authority specifically addresses health information.[149]

The authority of a personal representative applies only to the extent that PHI is relevant to the matters on which the personal representative is authorized to represent the individual. For example, if a person's authority to make health care decisions for an individual is limited to decisions regarding treatment for cancer, such person is a personal representative and must be treated as the individual with respect to PHI related to the cancer treatment of the individual, but may not be treated as the individual with respect to other PHI.[150]

b. Parents and Minors. In general, a person's right to control PHI is based on that person's right (under state or other applicable law) to control the health care itself. Because a parent usually has authority to make health care decisions about his or her minor child, a parent is generally a personal representative of his or her minor child under the Privacy Regulations and has the right to obtain access to health information about his or her minor child and exercise other such individual rights on behalf of the child. This would also be the case for a guardian or other person acting *in loco parentis* of a minor.[151]

There are exceptions in which a parent might not be the personal representative with respect to certain health information about a minor child, and the minor has the authority to

---

[147] 45 C.F.R. § 164.514(g).
[148] 45 C.F.R. § 164.502(g); 65 Fed. Reg. 82500.
[149] 65 Fed. Reg. 82500.
[150] 65 Fed. Reg. 82500.
[151] 45 C.F.R. §§ 164.502(g)(2), (g)(3); July 2001 Guidance.

act as an individual. In the following situations, the Privacy Regulations defer to determinations under other law that the parent does not control the minor's health care decisions and, thus, does not control the PHI related to that care.[152]

(i) When state or other law does not require consent of a parent before a minor can obtain a particular health care service, and the minor consents to the health care service, the parent is not the minor's personal representative under the Privacy Regulations. For example, when a state law provides an adolescent the right to consent to mental health treatment without the consent of his or her parent, and the adolescent obtains such treatment without the consent of the parent, the parent is not the personal representative under the Privacy Regulations for purposes of that treatment.

(ii) When a court or a person (other than the parent) authorized by law makes treatment decisions for a minor, the parent is not the personal representative of the minor for the relevant services. For example, courts may grant authority to make health care decisions for the minor to an adult other than the parent, or to the minor, or the court may make the decision(s) itself. In order to not undermine these court decisions, the parent is not the personal representative under the Privacy Regulations in these circumstances.

(iii) When a parent agrees to a confidential relationship between the minor and the provider, the parent does not have access to the health information related to that conversation or relationship.[153]

In addition, the Privacy Regulations do not preempt state law (including case law) specifically addressing disclosure of, or provision of access to, a minor's health information to a parent. This is true whether the state law permits, requires, or prohibits such disclosure or provision of access.[154] Thus, if a physician believes that disclosure of information about a minor would endanger that minor, but a state law requires disclosure to a parent, the physician may comply with the state law without violating the Privacy Regulations. Similarly, a provider may comply with a state law that requires disclosure to a parent and would not have to accommodate a request for confidential communications that would be contrary to state law.[155]

In the few cases in which the parent is not the personal representative of the minor, and state and other law about parental access is not explicit, a covered entity may provide or deny access to a parent provided that such discretion is permitted by state law or other law. The Privacy Regulations, thus, do not prevent a covered entity from providing access to a parent if the covered entity would have been able to provide this access under state law or other applicable law. This discretion to provide or deny access to a parent only may be exercised by a licensed health care professional, in the exercise of professional judgment.[156]

The Privacy Regulations defer to state law and reflect the DHHS position that issues related to the rights of parents and minors with respect to health care and PHI are best left to the states.[157]

c. Deceased Individuals. The PHI of a deceased individual is protected under the Privacy Regulations.[158] If under applicable law an executor, administrator, or other person has authority to act on behalf of a deceased individual or of the individual's estate, a covered entity must

---

[152] 45 C.F.R. §§ 164.502(g)(3).
[153] 45 C.F.R. § 164.502(g)(3); July 2001 Guidance.
[154] 45 C.F.R. § 164.502(g)(3)(ii).
[155] July 2001 Guidance.
[156] 45 C.F.R. § 164.502(g)(3)(ii)(C).
[157] 67 Fed. Reg. 53202.
[158] 45 C.F.R. § 164.502(f); 67 Fed. Reg. 53201.

treat such person as a personal representative of the deceased individual with respect to PHI relevant to such personal representation.[159]

The following other special provisions permit disclosure of PHI of deceased individuals.

(i) A covered entity may disclose PHI about a deceased individual to a law enforcement official for the purpose of alerting law enforcement of the death of the individual, if the covered entity has a suspicion that such death may have resulted from criminal conduct.[160]

(ii) A covered entity may disclose PHI to a coroner or medical examiner for the purpose of identifying a deceased individual, determining a cause of death, or other duties as authorized by law. A covered entity that also performs the duties of a coroner or medical examiner may use PHI for these purposes.[161]

(iii) A covered entity may disclose PHI to funeral directors, consistent with applicable law, as necessary to carry out their duties with respect to the decedent. If necessary for funeral directors to carry out their duties, the covered entity may disclose the PHI prior to, and in reasonable anticipation of, the individual's death.[162]

(iv) A covered entity may use PHI for, or disclose PHI to, organ procurement organizations or other entities engaged in the procurement, banking, or transplantation of cadaveric organs, eyes, or tissue for the purpose of facilitating organ, eye, or tissue donation and transplantation.[163]

(v) Special provisions apply to research on a decedent's information.[164]

d. Abuse, Neglect, Endangerment Situations. A covered entity may choose not to treat a person as the personal representative of the individual if the covered entity reasonably believes in his or her professional judgment that the individual has been or may be subjected to domestic violence, abuse, or neglect by such person, or that treating such person as the individual's personal representative could endanger the individual, and that it is not in the best interest of the individual to treat such person as the individual's personal representative.[165]

6. Incidental Disclosures

The Privacy Regulations are not intended to impede customary and necessary health care communications or practices, nor to require that all risk of incidental use or disclosure be eliminated to satisfy its standards.[166] The Privacy Regulations explicitly permit certain incidental uses and disclosures that occur as a result of a use or disclosure otherwise permitted by the Privacy Regulations.[167] Incidental uses or disclosures are permissible, however, only to the extent that the covered entity reasonably safeguards PHI to limit incidental uses and disclosures,[168] and implements the minimum necessary standard.[169]

For example, a health care provider may instruct an administrative staff member to bill a patient for a particular procedure, and may be overheard by one or more persons in the waiting room. Assuming that the provider made reasonable efforts to avoid being overheard

---

[159] 45 C.F.R. § 164.502(g)(4).
[160] 45 C.F.R. § 164.512(f)(4).
[161] 45 C.F.R. § 164.512(g)(1).
[162] 45 C.F.R. § 164.512(g)(2).
[163] 45 C.F.R. § 164.512(h).
[164] 45 C.F.R. § 164.512(i)(1)(iii).
[165] 45 C.F.R. § 164.502(g)(5).
[166] 67 Fed. Reg. 53194 (reiterating the July 2001 Guidance).
[167] 45 C.F.R. § 164.502(a)(1)(iii).
[168] 45 C.F.R. § 164.530(c)(2)(ii).
[169] 45 C.F.R. § 164.514(d).

and reasonably limited the information shared, an incidental disclosure resulting from such conversation is permissible under the Privacy Regulations.[170]

Other areas of concern addressed by this provision include:

- Health care providers engaging in confidential conversations with other providers or with patients, where there is a possibility that they could be overheard;
- Using sign-in sheets in waiting rooms;
- Maintaining patient charts at bedside;
- Using X-ray lightboards except in isolated areas;
- Not immediately destroying empty prescription vials;
- Individuals in a waiting room signing their names on a log sheet; and
- Calling out patient names in a waiting room.[171]

All of these actions and communications potentially involve incidental disclosures of PHI, but may nevertheless be permissible if reasonable safeguards are used to limit disclosure and minimum necessary standards are applied.

E. Administrative Requirements

To meet the requirements of HIPAA Privacy Regulations, a covered entity must create an organizational framework, which includes a privacy official, training policies and procedures, a system for reporting noncompliance, and other administrative requirements, as described in this section.[172]

1. Designation of Privacy Official and Contact Person

A covered entity must designate a privacy official who is responsible for the development and implementation of the policies and procedures of the covered entity. In addition, the covered entity must designate a contact person or office to be responsible for receiving complaints relating to the Privacy Regulations and to provide further information about matters covered by the covered entity's notice of privacy practices. These designations must be documented.[173] The contact person may, but need not be, the privacy official. Implementation is expected to vary widely, depending on the size and nature of the covered entity. Small entities may have a part-time privacy official, or may assign this as an additional duty to an existing staff person. In contrast, large organizations may have a full-time, dedicated privacy official.[174]

2. Training

A covered entity must train all members of its workforce (including volunteers, trainees, and others under direct control of the covered entity, whether paid or unpaid) on its policies and procedures with respect to PHI, as necessary and appropriate to their job functions. This training must initially be provided no later than the compliance date. Thereafter, each new

---

[170] 67 Fed. Reg. 53194.

[171] *See* 67 Fed. Reg. 53193 and 53195.

[172] These administrative requirements are very similar to the organizational efforts required to develop a corporate compliance program in accordance with guidelines issued by the DHHS Office of Inspector General (OIG). For information on how to integrate HIPAA compliance with a corporate compliance program, *see* Patricia I. Carter, *Applying Your Corporate Compliance Skills to the HIPAA Security Standard*, J. HEALTHCARE INFORMATION MGMT. 13 (Winter 2000); Patricia I. Carter, *Integrating HIPAA Privacy and Security into your Corporate Compliance Program*, paper presented at 2002 Annual Health Information Management Systems Society Conference, January 2002, *available at* www.himss.org/content/files/proceedings/2002/sessions/ses118.pdf.

[173] 45 C.F.R. § 164.530(a).

[174] *See* 65 Fed. Reg. 82561.

member of the workforce must be trained within a reasonable period of time after joining the covered entity's workforce. When there is a material change in a privacy policy or procedure, those whose jobs are affected must be retrained within a reasonable period of time. The covered entity must document that the required training has been provided.[175] The covered entity may determine the most effective means of achieving this training requirement for its workforce. Although not required under the Privacy Regulations, a covered entity may wish to have trainees sign a statement certifying that they received the privacy training and will honor all of the covered entity's privacy policies and procedures.

Training may also be advisable for individuals who are not members of the covered entities workforce but work closely with the covered entity. For example, for independent contractors, attendance at training sessions could be part of their contractual obligations. For a hospital's medical staff, attendance at training could be required under the medical staff by-laws as a condition of obtaining and maintaining clinical privileges.

3. Safeguards

A covered entity must have in place appropriate administrative, technical, and physical safeguards to protect the privacy of PHI, and reasonably safeguard it from any intentional or unintentional use or disclosure that is in violation of the Privacy Regulations.[176] These limitations are expected to work in conjunction with the minimum necessary rule, discussed in Section III, G.2. For electronic health information, this requirement is also expected to be coordinated with the HIPAA Security Regulations.[177]

These safeguards are intended to be scalable, because the nature of the required policies and procedures will vary with the size of the covered entity and the type of activities that the covered entity undertakes. A covered entity is not expected to guarantee the safety of PHI against all assaults. Circumvention of these safeguards may or may not signal a violation of the Privacy Regulations, depending on the circumstances and whether the covered entity had reasonable safeguards in place. Examples of appropriate safeguards include requiring that documents containing PHI be shredded prior to disposal, and requiring that doors to medical records departments (or to file cabinets housing such records) remain locked and limiting which personnel are authorized to have the key or key code.[178]

4. Complaints

Individuals have the right to make complaints to DHHS or to the covered entity concerning the covered entity's privacy policies and procedures or its compliance with the requirements of the Privacy Regulations. An individual may not be retaliated against for filing such a complaint.[179]

The covered entity must provide a process for individuals to make such complaints and must document all complaints received, and their disposition, if any.[180] No particular reporting mechanism is specified by the Privacy Regulations, and anonymous reporting is not required. The name of the contact person or office for such complaints, including a telephone number, must be provided in the covered entity's notice of privacy practices.[181] If a covered entity has a reporting mechanism in place as part of a corporate compliance program, that same mechanism can generally be used for reporting HIPAA-related complaints.

---

[175] 45 C.F.R. §§ 160.103; 164.530(b).
[176] 45 C.F.R. § 164.530(c).
[177] 65 Fed. Reg. 82561–82562. *See* Section IV regarding the proposed security regulations.
[178] 65 Fed. Reg. 82562.
[179] 45 C.F.R. §§ 164.520(b)(1)(vi) and 164.530(d). *See also* § 164.502(j)(1) regarding whistleblowers.
[180] 45 C.F.R. § 164.530(d).
[181] 45 C.F.R. § 164.520(b)(1)(vii).

5. Sanctions

A covered entity must have and apply appropriate sanctions against members of its workforce who fail to comply with the privacy policies and procedures of the covered entity or the requirements of the Privacy Regulations. Written policies and procedures must describe these sanctions, and any sanctions that are applied must be documented. These sanctions do not apply to whistleblower activities.[182]

In general, the HIPAA compliance program should set forth a progressive disciplinary policy for failing to comply with the organization's policies and procedures and applicable statutes and regulations. To the extent possible, this policy should be integrated with other disciplinary policies of the organization. Sanctions could range from oral warnings to suspension, termination, loss of clinical privileges, or financial penalties, as appropriate. Compliance policies should be consistently enforced, including, as appropriate, discipline of supervisors or managers for negligent failure to detect or correct an offense. Disciplinary policies and procedures should be communicated to all members of the workforce. Those affected should also be advised of the potential civil and criminal penalties for misuse or misappropriation of health information, and that such actions may be reported to law enforcement, regulatory, accreditation, and licensure organizations.

6. Duty to Mitigate

A covered entity must mitigate, to the extent practicable, any harmful effect known to the covered entity of a use or disclosure of PHI in violation of its policies and procedures or the requirements of the Privacy Regulations by the covered entity or its Business Associate.[183]

7. Refraining from Intimidating or Retaliatory Acts

A covered entity may not intimidate, threaten, coerce, discriminate against, or take other retaliatory action against:

a. Any individual for the exercise by the individual of any right under, or for participation by the individual in any process established by the Privacy Regulations in regard to his or her PHI, including the filing of a complaint;
b. Any individual or any other person for:
   - Filing of a complaint with DHHS;
   - Testifying, assisting, or participating in an investigation, compliance review, proceeding, or hearing under the Administrative Simplification provisions of HIPAA; or
   - Opposing any act or practice made unlawful by the Privacy Regulations, provided the individual or person has a good faith belief that the practice opposed is unlawful, and the manner of the opposition is reasonable and does not involve a disclosure of PHI in violation of the Privacy Regulations.[184]

8. Waiver of Rights

A covered entity may not require individuals to waive their rights to file complaints with DHHS as a condition of the provision of treatment, payment, enrollment in a health plan, or eligibility for benefits.[185]

---

[182] 45 C.F.R. § 164.530(e); 65 Fed. Reg. 82562.
[183] 45 C.F.R. § 164.530(f).
[184] 45 C.F.R. § 164.530(g).
[185] 45 C.F.R. § 164.530(h).

9. Policies and Procedures

A covered entity must implement policies and procedures with respect to PHI that are designed to comply with the Privacy Regulations. The policies and procedures must be reasonably designed, taking into account the size of and the type of activities that relate to PHI undertaken by the covered entity, to ensure such compliance. This reasonableness standard does not, however, permit or excuse an action that violates any other requirement of the Privacy Regulations.

Whenever there is a change in law that necessitates a change to the covered entity's policies or procedures, the covered entity must promptly document and implement the revised policy or procedure. If the change in law materially affects the content of the covered entity's notice of privacy practices, the notice must be promptly revised.

When a covered entity changes a privacy practice that is stated in the notice of privacy practices, and makes corresponding changes to its policies and procedures, it may make the changes effective for PHI that it created or received prior to the effective date of the notice revision, if the covered entity has included in its notice a statement reserving its right to make such a change. If a covered entity has not reserved its right to change a privacy practice that is stated in the notice, the covered entity is bound by the privacy practices as stated in the notice with respect to PHI created or received while such notice is in effect, and the change will affect only PHI created or received after the effective date of the revised notice. In either case, the covered entity may not implement a change to a policy or procedure prior to the effective date of the revised notice. A covered entity may make any other changes to policies and procedures at any time, if they do not materially affect the content of the notice, provided that the changes comply with the Privacy Regulations and are properly documented in advance of their effective date.[186]

10. Documentation

A covered entity must maintain the policies and procedures described in the preceding Section in written or electronic form. Other documentation requirements include:

- Notice (including all revisions);
- Documentation of the designated record set;
- Titles/offices of those responsible for processing requests for access, amendments and disclosures;
- Contents of an accounting of disclosures provided;
- Consents, authorizations, and related revocations;
- Documentation of resolutions of conflicts among authorizations;
- Training;
- Complaints received and their disposition; and
- Sanctions, including procedures and a record of sanctions applied.

If a communication is required by the Privacy Regulations to be in writing, the covered entity must maintain such writing, or an electronic copy, as documentation. If an action, activity, or designation is required by the Privacy Regulation to be documented, the covered entity must maintain a written or electronic record of such action, activity, or designation. A covered entity must retain these documents for six years from the date they were created or last in effect (the statute of limitations period for the civil monetary penalties).[187]

---

[186] 45 C.F.R. § 164.530(i).
[187] 45 C.F.R. § 164.530(j); 65 Fed. Reg. 82563.

F. Business Associates

The Privacy Regulations only apply directly to covered entities, but DHHS recognized that covered entities do not function in isolation, but use a variety of contractors, professional service providers, and other businesses in carrying out their health care activities. The Privacy Regulations permit covered entities to disclose PHI to these entities when such disclosure is necessary to help the covered entities carry out their health care functions, but not for the independent purposes of these business associates. The Privacy Regulations protect these disclosures, not by governing these business associates directly, but rather, by requiring that the covered entity obtain satisfactory written assurances that these business associates will use the information only for the purposes for which they were engaged by the covered entity, will safeguard the PHI from misuse, and will cooperate with and help the covered entity comply with the covered entity's responsibilities under the Privacy Regulations.[188]

1. Who is a Business Associate?

Not all outside vendors or service providers that have relationships with a covered entity are "business associates" for purposes of the Privacy Regulations. A business associate is a person or entity that performs functions on behalf of or provides certain services to the covered entity that involve the disclosure of PHI to the business associate for the business associate's use or further disclosure in performing services for the covered entity. A covered entity may be a business associate of another covered entity.[189]

Although they might otherwise meet the definition of a business associate, an exception is made and the business associate requirements do not apply to:

a. Disclosures by a covered entity to a health care provider for treatment of an individual (e.g., a hospital disclosing PHI to a member of its medical staff, or a physician disclosing PHI to a pharmacy to provide a prescription drug to an individual);[190]
b. Disclosures by group health plan, or health insurer or HMO with respect to a group health plan, to a plan sponsor, provided the plan document is amended and certain other requirements are met;[191]
c. Any member of the covered entity's workforce, which includes employees, volunteers, trainees, and other persons under the direct control of a covered entity, whether paid or unpaid. In a situation where the assigned work station of an independent contractor is on the covered entity's premises and such person performs a substantial proportion of his or her activities at that location, the covered entity may choose to treat this person either as a business associate or as part of its workforce. If there is no business associate contract, it will be assumed that this person is a member of the covered entity's workforce;[192]
d. A bank or other financial institution that does no more than process consumer-conducted financial transactions by debit, credit, or other payment card, clears checks, initiates or processes electronic funds transfers, or conducts any other activity that directly facilitates or effects the transfer of funds;[193]

---

[188] July 2001 Guidance; 45 C.F.R. §§ 164.103; 165.502(e) and 164.504(e).
[189] 45 C.F.R. § 164.504(e).
[190] 45 C.F.R. § 164.502(e)(1)(ii)(A).
[191] 45 C.F.R. § 164.502(e)(1)(ii)(B). See 45 C.F.R. § 164.504(f) and Section V regarding the group health plan requirements.
[192] 45 C.F.R. § 160.103; 65 Fed. Reg. 82480.
[193] 65 Fed. Reg. 82504–82505. But see www.hipaabanking.org regarding the efforts of the Banking Industry HIPAA Task Force, a joint initiative of NACHA (the Electronic Payments Association) and the American Bankers Association.

e. A person or organization that acts merely as a "conduit" for PHI (e.g., the U.S. Postal Service, private couriers, and electronic equivalents)—conduits simply transport information without accessing it other than on a random or infrequent basis as may be necessary for the performance of the transportation service or as required by law. Because no disclosure is intended by the covered entity and the probability of exposure to any PHI is small, no business associate relationship exists for HIPAA purposes;[194]

f. Health plans that are government programs providing public benefits; or[195]

g. Disclosures to a researcher for research purposes permitted by the Privacy Regulations.[196]

Examples of services that could give rise to a business associate relationship if they are performed on behalf of a covered entity and involve PHI, include:

- Billing;
- Language translation/interpretation;
- Transcription;
- Peer review;
- Accreditation;
- Quality assurance;
- Utilization review;
- Practice management;
- Claims processing or administration;
- Repricing of claims;
- Data analysis;
- Temporary staffing agencies; and
- Software vendors.

In addition, if the following types of services involve the disclosure of PHI from the covered entity, they would give rise to a business associate relationship:

- Legal;
- Actuarial;
- Accounting;
- Consulting;
- Data aggregation;
- Management;
- Administrative;
- Accreditation; and
- Financial.

A business associate contract is not required with persons or organizations whose functions, activities, or services do not involve the use or disclosure of PHI, and where any access to PHI by such persons would be minimal. For example, a health care provider is not required to enter into a business associate contract with its janitorial service because the performance of such service does not involve the use or disclosure of PHI, even though some minimal access to PHI may occur. In this case, where a janitor has contact with PHI incidentally, such disclosure is permissible as an incidental disclosure (see Section III.D.6), provided reasonable safeguards are in place.[197]

---

[194] 65 Fed. Reg. 82573
[195] 45 C.F.R. § 164.502(e)(1)(ii)(C).
[196] 67 Fed. Reg. 53252.
[197] 67 Fed. Reg. 53252–53253.

2. Business Associate Contracts—Contents

Business associates are not permitted to use or disclose PHI in ways that would not be permitted by the covered entity itself. A written contract is required between the covered entity and the business associate that limits the business associate's uses and disclosures of PHI to those permitted by the contract and imposes certain security, inspection and reporting requirements on the business associate. The following specific contract provisions are set forth in the Privacy Regulations.[198] A sample annotated business associate contract may be found in Appendix A. The business associate contract must contain provisions that:

a. Establish the permitted and required uses and disclosure of PHI by the business associate. While the contract need not detail each and every permitted use or disclosure of PHI, the contract should state the main purpose(s) for which the business associate may use or disclose PHI and generally indicate the reasons and types of persons to whom the business associate may make further disclosures.

A business associate may not use or disclose PHI to the extent such use or disclosure would not be permitted if done by the covered entity except that a business associate can specifically:

(i) Use the PHI for proper management/administration of the business associate and to carry out the legal responsibilities of the business associate; PHI may also be disclosed for these purposes: (A) if the disclosure is required by law; or (B) the business associate: (1) obtains reasonable assurances from the person to whom the information is disclosed that it will be held confidential and used or further disclosed only as required by law or for the purposes for which it was disclosed to the person; and (2) is notified by the person of any instances of which he or she is aware in which the confidentiality of the information has been breached.

(ii) Disclose the PHI for data aggregation services relating to the health care operations of the covered entity.

b. Explicitly provide that the business associate has the obligation to:

(i) Not use or further disclose PHI other than as permitted or required by the contract or as required by law;

(ii) Use appropriate safeguards to prevent use or disclosure of PHI other than as provided for by its contract;

(iii) Report to the covered entity any use or disclosure of PHI not provided for by its contract of which the business associate becomes aware;

(iv) Ensure that any agents (including subcontractors) to whom the business associate provides PHI agrees to the same restrictions and conditions that apply to the business associate with respect to such information;

(v) Make available PHI to individuals in accordance with the Privacy Regulations' provisions regarding individual access;

(vi) Make available PHI for amendment and incorporate any amendments to the PHI in accordance with the Privacy Regulations' provisions regarding an individual's right to have a covered entity amend PHI;

(vii) Make available an accounting of disclosures in accordance with the Privacy Regulations' provisions regarding an individual's right to receive an accounting of certain disclosures of his or her PHI made by the covered entity (or its business associates);

(viii) Make available to DHHS the business associate's internal practices, books, and records relating to the use and disclosure of PHI received from or created on behalf

---

[198] 45 C.F.R. § 164.504(e).

of the covered entity for purposes of determining the covered entity's compliance; and

    (ix) Return to the covered entity, or destroy, all PHI at the termination of the contract so that the business associate maintains no copies of the information in any form. If such return or destruction is not feasible (e.g., aggregated data in backup files or retention required by other law), extend the protections of the contract to the retained information and limit further uses and disclosures to those purposes that make the return or destruction of the information infeasible.

c. Authorize termination of the services contract and business associate contract by the covered entity, if the covered entity determines that the business associate has violated a material term of the business associate contract.

If both the covered entity and its business associate are governmental entities, special provisions apply. A memorandum of understanding is used in lieu of a business associate contract.[199]

3. Business Associate Contracts—Deadlines

The covered entity must have executed a valid business associate agreement with each of its business associates on or before the compliance date, except that this deadline is extended under the circumstances described below. It is important to note, however, that despite this additional time allowed for negotiating business associate agreements, the covered entity is still responsible for: (a) making information available to DHHS, including information held by a business associate, as necessary for DHHS to determine compliance by the covered entity; (b) complying with individuals' rights with respect to accessing or amending their PHI held by a business associate, or receiving an accounting of disclosures by a business associate; and (c) mitigating, to the extent practicable, any harmful effect that is known to the covered entity of a use or disclosure of PHI by its business associate in violation of the covered entity's policies and procedures or the requirements of the Privacy Regulations.[200] Therefore, the covered entity may conclude that it is desirable to enter into business associate agreements with all of its business associates by the compliance date, so the business associates are contractually obligated to immediately support the covered entity's compliance efforts in this regard.

The transition provision provides that covered entities, other than small health plans, may continue to operate under certain existing contracts with business associates for up to one year beyond the April 14, 2003, compliance date. This additional transition period is available for a written contract with a business associate in effect prior to October 15, 2002, provided that the contract is not renewed or modified prior to April 14, 2003. These qualifying contracts must be amended to include the required business associate provisions by the earlier of April 14, 2004, or the date the contract is renewed or otherwise modified. (The automatic renewal of "evergreen" contracts, which renew without action or modification, is not considered a "renewal" for purposes of this transition provision.) These transition provisions provide covered entities with the flexibility to incorporate the business associate contract pro-visions at the time they would otherwise modify or renew an existing services contract. Any oral agreement, or any written agreement entered into on or after October 15, 2003, does not qualify for this special treatment and a valid business associate contract is required by April 14, 2003. For small health plans, the compliance date is April 14, 2004, and is not impacted by this transition provision.[201]

---

[199] 45 C.F.R. § 164.502(e)(3).
[200] 45 C.F.R. § 164.532(d); 67 Fed. Reg. 53250.
[201] 45 C.F.R. § 164.532(d); 67 Fed. Reg. 53250.

4. Enforcement

The covered entity does not have a duty to actively monitor its business associates' actions and is not responsible or liable for the actions of its business associates.[202] Nevertheless, the covered entity is expected to investigate when it receives complaints or other information that contain substantial and credible evidence of violation by a business associate, and it must act upon any knowledge of such violation that it possesses.[203] DHHS will view a covered entity that has substantial and credible evidence of a violation as "knowing" of such violation.

A covered entity that knows of a pattern of activity or practice of the business associate that constitutes a material breach or violation of the business associate's obligations under the contract or other arrangement, must take reasonable steps to cure the breach or end the violation, and if such steps are unsuccessful, must either terminate the contract or arrangement, if feasible; or if termination is not feasible, report the problem to DHHS. Termination is "not feasible" when terminating the contract would be "unreasonably burdensome" on the covered entity or when there are "no viable alternatives" to continuing a contract with that particular business associate. Termination is regarded as feasible even if it may inconvenience the covered entity or cost the covered entity more money to contract with other potential business associates.[204]

A business associate that violates these terms is generally not subject to HIPAA penalties (unless the business associate is also a covered entity). However, a covered entity could pursue legal action against a business associate and recover damages (ordinary and consequential) for the business associate's breach of the business associate contract. A covered entity may also include an indemnification clause in the contract that requires the business associate to indemnify the covered entity for any penalties or fines the covered entity receives as a result of a violation by the business associate.

G. Other Key Concepts

1. Organizational Structure

A covered entity has some options under the Privacy Regulations in terms of how it establishes its organizational structure for compliance purposes:

a. *Hybrid Entity*: A hybrid entity is a single legal entity whose business activities include both covered and non-covered functions, and chooses to elect hybrid status by designating and documenting its health care component.[205] A hybrid entity might include, for example, a residential services organization that only incidentally provides health care services to its residents; a drugstore that includes both a pharmacy and a "front end" store that sells general merchandise; or a manufacturing company that runs an on-site medical clinic for employees.

The health care component must include any component that would meet the definition of a covered entity if it were a separate legal entity. The health care component may only include a component that performs covered functions, or a component that performs activities that would make it a business associate if it were a separate legal entity.[206]

---

[202] 67 Fed. Reg. 53252.
[203] 65 Fed. Reg. 82505.
[204] 45 C.F.R. § 164.504(e)(1)(2); 65 Fed. Reg. 82505.
[205] 45 C.F.R. § 164.504(a) and (c). Covered Functions are defined at 45 C.F.R. § 164.501 as those functions of a covered entity the performance of which makes the entity a health plan, health care provider, or health care clearinghouse.
[206] 45 C.F.R. § 164.504(c)(3)(iii).

If the covered entity is a hybrid entity, the Privacy Regulations apply to only the health care component. The covered entity must ensure that the health care component complies with the applicable requirements of the regulations.[207] A hybrid entity is required to create adequate separation, in the form of "firewalls," between the health care component(s) and other components of the entity. Transfer of PHI held by the health care component to other components of the hybrid entity is a disclosure under the Privacy Regulations, and, thus, allowed only to the same extent such a disclosure is permitted to a separate entity.[208]

Covered entities that do not choose to elect hybrid status by designating health care component(s) are subject to the Privacy Regulations in their entirety. If a covered entity does not choose to be a hybrid entity, it is not required to erect firewalls around its health care functions; however, the entity still only is allowed to use PHI as permitted by the Privacy Regulations. For example, workforce members may be permitted access to PHI only as necessary to carry out their duties with respect to the entity's covered functions.[209]

b. *Affiliated Entities*: Legally separate covered entities that are affiliated (i.e., under common ownership or control) may designate themselves as a single covered entity for purposes of compliance with the Privacy Regulations. This designation must be documented. If combining functions of provider and health plan (and/or clearinghouse), each affiliate must comply with the requirements applicable to its type of covered entity.[210]

c. *Organized Health Care Arrangement*: Certain covered entities may act jointly as part of an organized health care arrangement (OHCA). Such an arrangement does not mean that the covered entities are combined for all purposes, but does permit use of combined notice of privacy practices and acknowledgments. The definition of an OHCA includes the following five types of arrangements:

(i) A clinically integrated care setting in which individuals typically receive health care from more than one health care provider;

(ii) An organized system of health care in which more than one covered entity participates, and in which the participating covered entities hold themselves out to the public as participating in a joint arrangement, and participate in certain joint activities;

(iii) A group health plan and a health insurance issuer or HMO with respect to such group health plan, but only with respect to the group health plan members' PHI;

(iv) Multiple group health plans maintained by the same plan sponsor; or

(v) Group health plans, and health insurance issuers or HMOs through which such plans are funded and administered.[211]

2. Minimum Necessary

Reasonable steps must be taken to limit uses and disclosures to the minimum amount of PHI required to accomplish the intended purpose.[212] The idea is to avoid using or disclosing the individual's entire health record unless this is truly necessary, and to make covered entities evaluate their practices and limit the amount of information used or disclosed as appropriate to the circumstances.

There are exceptions to the minimum necessary rule. The requirement does not apply to disclosures to a health care provider for treatment purposes; disclosures to individuals of their

---

[207] 45 C.F.R. § 164.504(a)–(c).
[208] 67 Fed. Reg. 53205.
[209] 67 Fed. Reg. 53205.
[210] 45 C.F.R. § 164.504(a), (d).
[211] 45 C.F.R. § 164.501; *see also* 45 C.F.R. § 164.520(d) (joint notice) and 45 C.F.R. § 164.506(f) (joint consent)
[212] 45 C.F.R. § 164.502(b); July 2001 Guidance.

own PHI; uses or disclosures under an authorization; disclosures to DHHS regarding compliance or enforcement; or, uses and disclosures required by law.[213]

A covered entity must determine the persons or classes of persons within the covered entity who need access to PHI to carry out their job duties, the categories or types of PHI needed, and conditions appropriate to such access. A covered entity must develop policies and procedures for uses and disclosures that identify the amount of information that is required. For example, a hospital may implement policies that permit doctors, nurses, or others involved in treatment to have access to the entire medical record. When access to the entire medical record is necessary, the policy should state this explicitly and provide the justification. For routine and recurring disclosure situations, the policies and procedures may be standard protocols. For non-routine uses and disclosures, the covered entity must develop reasonable criteria for making the determination as to what will be considered the minimum necessary information for the specific purpose, and review disclosures on an individual basis in accordance with these criteria.[214]

In certain circumstances, a covered entity may rely on the judgment of the party requesting the disclosure as to the minimum amount of information that is needed. Such reliance must be reasonable under the particular circumstances of the request. This reliance is permitted when the request is made by:

- A public official, for a disclosure permitted 45 C.F.R. § 164.512 (e.g., public health disclosures or disclosures for law enforcement), if the public official represents that the amount requested is the minimum required for the purpose;
- Another covered entity, because covered entities are required to limit their requests to what they determine to be the minimum necessary information for the purpose;
- A professional who is a workforce member or business associate of the covered entity, for the purpose of providing professional services, if the professional represents that this amount requested is the minimum required for the purpose; or
- A researcher with appropriate documentation from an Institutional Review Board (IRB) or Privacy Board.[215]

The Privacy Regulations do not require such reliance on another party's determination, however, and the covered entity retains the right to make its own minimum necessary determination for disclosures to which the minimum necessary standard applies.[216]

3. Verification

Prior to any disclosure permitted under the Privacy Regulations, the covered entity must verify the identity and authority of the person requesting the PHI, and obtain any required documentation associated with the request.[217]

---

[213] 45 C.F.R. § 164.502(b); July 2001 Guidance.
[214] 45 C.F.R. § 164.514(d); July 2001 Guidance.
[215] 45 C.F.R. § 164.514(d).
[216] 45 C.F.R. § 164.514(d); July 2001 Guidance.
[217] 45 C.F.R. § 164.514(h).

IV. PROPOSED SECURITY REGULATIONS

The proposed Security Regulations require reasonable and appropriate administrative, technical, and physical safeguards that insure the integrity, availability, and confidentiality of health care information, and protect against reasonably foreseeable threats to the security or integrity of the information.[1] The proposed regulations include technical guidance as well as administrative requirements for those who maintain or transmit electronic health information.

Like the Privacy Regulations, the Security Regulations are intended to be scalable and flexible. No specific technologies are required. Covered entities are expected to have different security needs, depending on their size and complexity. The Security Regulations require each covered entity to assess its potential risks and vulnerabilities and its own security needs. The scalability and flexibility of the regulations allow covered entities to adopt security plans that fit their organizations; yet, that scalability and flexibility also leaves covered entities at risk for making an erroneous judgment about their vulnerabilities, or making the wrong business decision in their investment in technology and development of their security management plan. There are no pre-determined "safe harbors" to illustrate the "right" level of security protections for a particular organization. Fortunately, the proposed regulations are consistent with common sense and good information systems practices that most organizations should be following anyway.

The standards are divided into four (somewhat overlapping) categories, as shown below. The number of requirements in each category is noted in the parentheses.

Administrative procedures (12 standards)	Physical safeguards (6 standards)
To guard data integrity, confidentiality, and availability. These are documented, formal practices for selecting and executing information security measures to protect data, and staff responsibilities for the protection of data.	To guard data integrity, confidentiality, and availability. These safeguards relate to the protection of the physical computer system, and related buildings and equipment, from fire and other environmental hazards. Also included are the use of locks, keys, and administrative measures to control access to computer systems and facilities.

Technical data security services (5 standards)	Technical security mechanisms (1 standard)
To guard data integrity, confidentiality, and availability. These include the processes used to protect, control and monitor information access.	To prevent unauthorized access to data transmitted over a communications network.

---

[1] 63 Fed. Reg. 43249.

A. Administrative Procedures

1. Certification

Each covered entity is required to evaluate its computer systems and network designs and certify that appropriate security measures have been implemented. This evaluation could be performed internally or by an external accrediting agency.[2] A knowledgeable staff person could do this evaluation and certification internally, perhaps with the assistance of a consultant or the vendor of the practice management system. If entering into a contract with a software vendor, consider including a provision that obligates the vendor to assist in the certification process.

2. Chain of Trust Partner Agreement

If a covered entity's data are processed through an outside party, the covered entity must enter into a "chain of trust" partner agreement with that outside party. This is a contract in which the parties agree to electronically exchange data and to protect the transmitted data. The sender and receiver are each required to depend on the other to maintain the integrity and confidentiality of the transmitted information. Multiple chain of trust agreements may be involved in moving information from the originating party to the ultimate receiving party. For example, a provider may contract with a clearinghouse to transmit claims to the clearinghouse; the clearinghouse, in turn, may contract with another clearinghouse or with a health plan for the further transmittal of those claims. At each transmitted point, chain of trust agreements are required so that the same level of security will be maintained at all links in the chain when information moves from one organization to another.[3]

When the final Security Regulations are issued, this chain of trust concept is likely to be "harmonized" with the Privacy Regulations and become more similar to the business associate requirements.

3. Contingency Plan

A covered entity must have a contingency plan for responding to system emergencies, such as fires, power failures, or system "crashes," or other system unavailability. The organization is required to take steps such as performing periodic backups of data, having alternate facilities available for continuing critical operations in the event of an emergency, and having disaster recovery procedures in place. To satisfy the requirement, this contingency plan needs to include the following:

- A criticality analysis of application programs and data files to determine how critical to continued operations each one is;
- A data backup plan;
- A disaster recovery plan;
- An emergency mode operation plan; and
- Testing and revision procedures.[4]

4. Formal Mechanism for Processing Records

A formal mechanism for processing records is required; that is, documented policies and procedures for the routine and nonroutine receipt, manipulation, storage, dissemination,

---

[2]63 Fed. Reg. 43251 (proposed 45 C.F.R. § 142.308(a)(1)).
[3]63 Fed. Reg. 43252 (proposed 45 C.F.R. § 142.308(a)(2)).
[4]63 Fed. Reg. 43252 (proposed 45 C.F.R. § 142.308(a)(3)).

transmission, and/or disposal of health information.[5] Thinking through and documenting such processes in advance should help limit the inadvertent loss or disclosure of secure information because of poor process issues. Confidentiality policies should be implemented that state the types of information considered confidential; the individuals authorized to release confidential information; the procedures that must be followed to release information; and the types of individuals who are authorized to receive confidential information.

5. Information Access Control

A covered entity must establish and maintain formal, documented policies and procedures for granting different levels of access to health care information. To satisfy this requirement, the following features should be contained in the organization's policies and procedures:

- Access authorization;
- Access establishment; and
- Access modification.

This means developing administrative procedures for determining what access individuals should have, giving them that access, and updating that access as the situation changes.[6] A covered entity should formulate and document policies and procedures for determining each user's level of access to records. Determinations of a person's access privileges should be thought out in advance, not made on an ad hoc basis at the time of assigning those privileges.

Users should have only as much access to view or manipulate records as is legitimately required by their job functions. Authorization levels can include different combinations of authority to view, edit, add, delete, and print records. Printing may be restricted to maintain control over data that might be removed from the premises. Deletion of records should be restricted so that no one can delete files until the appropriate retention period has expired. System software should allow corrections to be appended to the record, without deleting the original information.

Methods of providing this predetermined level of access are discussed under Technical Data Security Services, in Section IV.C.1.

6. Internal Audit

There must be an ongoing internal audit process, which involves an in-house review of the records of system activity (e.g., logins, file accesses, security incidents) maintained by the covered entity.[7] This is important in enabling the organization to identify potential security violations.

Audit trails provide a record of who has accessed files and who is responsible for changes, deletions, etc., that have been made. Any use of an "override" function to access records should be included in the audit trail. Audit trails help identify the user when unauthorized access occurs. Publicizing the fact that all access to records will be documented can help deter unauthorized users and improper use.

7. Personnel Security

All personnel with access to health information must be authorized to access this information only after receiving appropriate clearances. This is important to prevent unnecessary or inadvertent access to secure information. Covered entities must satisfy the following requirements.

---

[5] 63 Fed. Reg. 43252 (proposed 45 C.F.R. § 142.308(a)(4)).
[6] 63 Fed. Reg. 43252 (proposed 45 C.F.R. § 142.308(a)(5)).
[7] 63 Fed. Reg. 43252 (proposed 45 C.F.R. § 142.308(a)(6)).

- Assure supervision of personnel performing technical systems maintenance activities by authorized, knowledgeable persons.
- Maintain access authorization records.
- Insure that operating, and in some cases, maintenance personnel have proper access.
- Employ personnel clearance procedures.
- Employ personnel security policies/procedures.
- Ensure that system users, including technical maintenance personnel, are trained in system security.[8]

8. Security Configuration Management

A covered entity must implement security measures for its information system(s), and these measures must be coordinated and integrated with other system configuration management practices. These procedures allow the covered entity to create and manage system security and integrity, and to ensure that routine changes to system hardware and/or software do not contribute to or create security weaknesses. This requirement includes the following:

- Documentation of system security measures;
- Hardware/software installation and maintenance review and testing for security features;
- Inventory procedures (i.e., knowing what hardware and software is and should be on your system—and what should not be);
- Security testing (e.g., after installing, changing, or removing hardware or software); and
- Virus checking.[9]

9. Security Incident Procedures

Security incident procedures must be implemented, so that security violations are reported and handled promptly and appropriately. These are formal, documented instructions for reporting security breaches, and must include the following:

- Reporting procedures; and
- Response procedures.[10]

A covered entity should establish and communicate a procedure for employees and others to confidentially report suspected (or detected) security breaches. This procedure should make it clear that no adverse action will be taken against anyone for making such a report. Mechanisms for making reports anonymously can encourage reporting.

Some security breaches have come to light through media attention, and the surrounding publicity can be damaging to an organization. A covered entity may wish to consider preparing a public relations response plan as part of its response procedure for use in the event of a security breach.

10. Security Management Process

The Security Regulations require that a covered entity develop a process for security management. This involves creating, administering, and overseeing policies to ensure the prevention, detection, containment, and correction of security breaches. The rules require the organization to have a formal security management process in place to address the full range of

---

[8] 63 Fed. Reg. 43252 (proposed 45 C.F.R. § 142.308(a)(7)).
[9] 63 Fed. Reg. 43252 (proposed 45 C.F.R. § 142.308(a)(8)).
[10] 63 Fed. Reg. 43252 (proposed 45 C.F.R. § 142.308(a)(9)).

security issues. Security management includes the following mandatory implementation features:

- Risk analysis;
- Risk management;
- A sanction policy; and
- A security policy (high level policy).[11]

11. Termination Procedures

A covered entity must implement termination procedures, which are formal, documented instructions, including appropriate security measures, for the cancellation of access authority of an employee or an internal/external user, such as upon termination of employment or termination of a contract. These procedures are important to prevent the possibility of unauthorized access to secure data by those who are no longer authorized to access it. Termination procedures must include the following mandatory implementation features:

- Changing combination locks;
- Removal from access lists;
- Removal of user accounts/passwords; and
- Collecting keys, tokens, or cards that allow access.[12]

Once an employee terminates, access should be immediately deactivated. Disgruntled employees and former employees are among the greatest risks to any computer system. Covered entities should also be aware of unusual downloading activity that may indicate the theft of information.

12. Training

All staff must receive security training regarding the vulnerabilities of the health information in a covered entity's possession and the procedures that must be followed to ensure the protection of that information. This is important because employees need to understand their security responsibilities and make security a part of their day-to-day activities. Staff training needs to include the following:

- Awareness training for all personnel, including management (this is also included as a requirement under the Physical Safeguards provisions);
- Periodic security reminders (regarding the importance of confidentiality and data security);
- User education concerning protection against viruses;
- User education regarding the importance of monitoring login success/failure, and how to report discrepancies; and
- User education in password management.[13]

A covered entity should make sensitivity to confidentiality issues part of the employee's job requirements. The ability to maintain confidentiality should be a factor in the hiring process and included in job descriptions. Knowledge of and adherence to confidentiality and security policies should also be a factor in employee evaluations (and employees should be advised of

---

[11] 63 Fed. Reg. 43252 (proposed 45 C.F.R. § 142.308(a)(10)).
[12] 63 Fed. Reg. 43252 (proposed 45 C.F.R. § 142.308(a)(11)).
[13] 63 Fed. Reg. 43252 (proposed 45 C.F.R. § 142.308(a)(12)).

this in advance). By linking performance reviews to confidentiality and security policies, employees will recognize the importance of these issues to the organization and have an ongoing incentive to adhere to the organization's policies, thereby helping to prevent unauthorized disclosures.

B. Physical Safeguards

1. Assigned Security Responsibility

Security responsibilities should be assigned to a specific individual or organization, and the assignment should be documented. The responsibilities of this position (commonly referred to as the Security Officer) include the management and supervision of: (i) the use of security measures to protect data; and (ii) the conduct of personnel in relation to the protection of data.[14] This assignment is important to provide an organizational focus for security issues, emphasize the importance of security, and to pinpoint responsibility.

2. Media Controls

Media controls are required in the form of formal, documented policies and procedures that govern the receipt and removal of hardware/software (e.g., disks, diskettes, tapes) in and out of a facility. They are important to ensure total control of storage media containing health information. These controls include the following mandatory implementation features:

- Controlled access to media;
- Accountability (tracking mechanism);
- Data backup;
- Data storage; and
- Disposal.[15]

Media controls could include establishing procedures regarding an outside vendor picking up and/or storing data backups off-site, including assuring that the vendor has signed a confidentiality agreement and agreed to certain record retention policies. Media controls should also be in place, for example, when disposing of outdated equipment (such as an old computer) that contains confidential information. It is not sufficient to delete the files from the computer's hard disk. The disk must be erased with special demagnetizing equipment (e.g., a "degausser") or scrubbed with special software that overwrites the data areas a prescribed number of times; otherwise, the information will still be recoverable. Similar precautions should be taken when disposing of old backup media.

3. Physical Access Controls

Formal, documented policies and procedures are required that limit physical access while ensuring that properly authorized access is permitted. These controls are extremely important to the security of health information by preventing unauthorized physical access to information and ensuring that authorized personnel have proper access. These physical access controls must include the following mandatory implementation features:

- Disaster recovery;
- Emergency mode operation;

---

[14] 63 Fed. Reg. 43253 (proposed 45 C.F.R. § 142.308(b)(1)).
[15] 63 Fed. Reg. 43253 (proposed 45 C.F.R. § 142.308(b)(2)).

- Equipment control (into and out of site);
- A facility security plan;
- Procedures for verifying access authorizations prior to physical access;
- Maintenance records;
- Need-to-know procedures for personnel access;
- Sign-in for visitors and escort, if appropriate; and
- Testing and revision.[16]

Laptops, personal digital assistants (PDA), and other handheld computers are particularly susceptible to theft, and the theft of the device includes all of the confidential information that it might contain. Particular care should be taken with the use and storage of these portable computers. Consider additional security measures, such as anti-theft devices, password-controlled access, and encryption of data.

4. Policy/Guideline on Workstation Use

A covered entity must have documented procedures on workstation use, which explain the proper functions to be performed and the manner in which those functions are to be performed (e.g., logging off before leaving a terminal unattended).[17] This is important so that employees will understand the manner in which workstations must be used to maximize the security of health information.

A covered entity's documented procedures should include sanctions for individuals who share their passwords/identifiers or fail to log off their workstations. Workstations should not be left unattended while logged in. Most computer workstations can be programmed to log off automatically or revert to a password-protected screensaver if not used for a predetermined period of time.

5. Secure Workstation Location

A covered entity is required to establish physical safeguards to eliminate or minimize the possibility of unauthorized access to information by placing workstations in appropriate locations.[18] This is especially important in areas where there is patient and visitor traffic.

Servers can be located in locked locations accessible only to authorized personnel. Most workstations need to be more accessible than that. Nevertheless, computer terminals should be located in areas that limit viewing or access by unauthorized users. Face computer screens away from public areas, use privacy screens, and/or have a counter or other barrier between the computer terminal and the public area. For example, avoid placing computer terminals used to access patient data in a location facing the public reception area in a physician's office.

6. Security Awareness Training

Security awareness training is required for all employees, agents, and contractors.[19] This is important because they need to understand their security responsibilities based on their job functions in the organization and make security a part of their daily activities.

Software that automatically reminds users of security measures as they log onto the system helps to reinforce the importance of security and confidentiality. These reminders should vary randomly, to keep the message fresh.

---

[16] 63 Fed. Reg. 43253 (proposed 45 C.F.R. § 142.308(b)(3)).
[17] 63 Fed. Reg. 43253 (proposed 45 C.F.R. § 142.308(b)(4)).
[18] 63 Fed. Reg. 43253 (proposed 45 C.F.R. § 142.308(b)(5)).
[19] 63 Fed. Reg. 43253 (proposed 45 C.F.R. § 142.308(b)(6)).

C. Technical Data Security Services

1. Access Control

Access control is required in order to restrict access to resources and allow access only by authorized entities/persons. A balance between accessibility and security is needed. People must have access to the information they need to provide treatment and to perform other necessary activities, but it is equally important to limit health information access to those members of the workforce who have a legitimate business need for it. Types of access control include mandatory access control, discretionary access control, time-of-day restrictions, classification, and subject-object separation. A procedure for emergency access is required. In addition, at least one of the following three implementation features is required to control access:

- Context-based access;
- Role-based access; or
- User-based access.[20]

In a small organization, user-based control is the most common. Each user is given individualized access to those functions he or she needs to perform necessary job duties. In a larger organization, role-based access, with access determined by the individual's job classification, may be more practical. The job classifications should be as specific as possible. For example, all nurses in a medical facility probably do not need the same set of access privileges; for example, consider the different information needs of a nurse with administrative duties, as compared to a nurse providing patient care only.

2. Audit Controls

Each covered entity is required to put in place audit control mechanisms to record and examine system activity.[21] These controls help the organization identify suspect data access activities, assess its security program, and respond to potential weaknesses.

3. Authorization Control

A mechanism for obtaining consent for the use and disclosure of health information is required. These controls are necessary to ensure that health information is used only by properly authorized individuals. Either of the following implementation features may be used:

- Role-based access; or
- User-based access (*see* Section IV.C.1).[22]

4. Data Authentication

A covered entity must be able to corroborate that data in its possession has not been altered or destroyed in an unauthorized manner.[23] Examples of how data corroboration may be assured include the use of a check sum, double keying, a message authentication code, or digital signature. This requirement appears to apply only to data being transmitted (not just being stored or maintained).

---

[20] 63 Fed. Reg. 43254 (proposed 45 C.F.R. § 142.308(c)(1)).
[21] 63 Fed. Reg. 43254 (proposed 45 C.F.R. § 142.308(c)(2)).
[22] 63 Fed. Reg. 43254 (proposed 45 C.F.R. § 142.308(c)(3)).
[23] 63 Fed. Reg. 43254 (proposed 45 C.F.R. § 142.308(c)(4)).

5. Entity Authentication

Procedures for entity authentication (which corroborate that an entity is who it claims to be) must be implemented. Authentication is important to prevent the improper identification of an entity that is accessing secure data. The following implementation features must be used:

- Automatic log off; and
- Unique user identification.

In addition, at least one of the following implementation features must be used:

- A biometric identification system (e.g., fingerprints, voiceprints, or retina scan);
- A password system;
- A personal identification number (PIN);
- Telephone callback, in which senders and receivers of data are identified through a series of exchanges of identifying codes ("questions and answers"); or
- A token system that uses a physical device for user identification (e.g., a security card and a card reader).[24]

D. Technical Security Mechanisms

A covered entity that uses communications or communication networks is required to protect transmissions containing health information that are sent electronically over open networks so that they cannot be easily intercepted and interpreted by parties other than the intended recipient, and to protect their information systems from intruders trying to access the systems through external communication portals. When using open networks (such as the Internet), some form of encryption should be employed. The utilization of less open systems/networks such as those provided by a value-added network (VAN) or private-wire arrangement provides sufficient access controls to allow encryption to be an optional feature. These security controls are important because of the potential for compromise of data being transmitted over open communication systems.

The following two implementation features are required:

- Integrity controls; and
- Message authentication.

Plus, one of the following implementation features is also required:

- Access controls; or
- Encryption.

In addition, if using a network for communications, the following implementation features are required:

- Alarm;
- Audit trail;
- Entity authentication; and
- Event reporting.[25]

---

[24] 63 Fed. Reg. 43254 (proposed 45 C.F.R. § 142.308(c)(5)).
[25] 63 Fed. Reg. 43255 (proposed 45 C.F.R. § 142.308(d)).

E. Electronic Signatures

As a "companion" regulation to the proposed Security Regulations, DHHS issued proposed regulations establishing digital signatures as the standard for electronic signatures in health care.[26] DHHS has announced that it does not intend to issue final regulations based on those proposed regulations. The standards and technology in this area are still developing. As a result, the proposed electronic signature standards are not discussed in this book.

F. Integration of Privacy and Security

Although the Security Regulations are still in proposed form, covered entities should be familiarizing themselves with the requirements and beginning to plan their implementation. For the most part, the Security Regulations represent "best practices," and DHHS has stated that they are not expected to change significantly when finalized.

Moreover, the Privacy Regulations require the following:

> Standard: safeguards. A covered entity must have in place appropriate administrative, technical, and physical safeguards to protect the privacy of protected health information. 45 C.F.R. § 164.530(c)(1).

Compliance with the Privacy Regulations will therefore require covered entities to implement appropriate safeguards for all forms of PHI; the Security Regulations can provide guidance on what are considered appropriate safeguards for PHI in electronic form.

---

[26] 63 Fed. Reg. 43256.

V. EMPLOYER-SPONSORED HEALTH PLANS

A. Applicability

When HIPAA first became law, employers concentrated on the provisions relating to special enrollment periods, certificates of creditable coverage and other provisions of Title I of HIPAA relating to the portability of coverage. Now employer attention needs to shift to the Administrative Simplification provisions under Title II.

Health plans, including employer-sponsored group health plans, are covered entities. Employers are not directly subject to the regulations; however, most employers sponsor employee health plans that are covered entities. The employer is often not only the plan sponsor, but may also be the plan administrator and plan fiduciary under the Employee Retirement Income Security Act of 1974 (ERISA). HIPAA recognizes that, under ERISA, a plan and its plan sponsor are separate legal entities. But, in practical terms, it is the plan sponsor that typically acts on behalf of the plan, because the plan has no employees of its own. Therefore, it is the employer, as the plan sponsor and fiduciary, that will have to be responsible for assuring the plan's compliance with the HIPAA regulations. Employers offering self-insured health plans will be the most directly affected and will be responsible for the plan's full compliance with the HIPAA regulations, even if they use a third party administrator (TPA). Employers offering fully insured plans will be able to delegate many compliance functions to the insurer but will retain some responsibilities, particularly if using or creating PHI.

B. Covered Plans

A health plan is a covered entity if it is an individual or group plan that provides or pays the cost of medical care. This broad definition of health plan includes employee welfare plans (as defined by ERISA) that offer health care benefits, whether insured or self-insured. An exception is made for group health plans that have fewer than 50 participants and are administered by the employer (i.e., not by a third party). Covered group health plans include, for example: medical plans, dental plans, vision plans, health flexible spending accounts, and some employee assistance plans (EAP). Disability (income replacement) plans, life insurance plans, and workers' compensation plans are not covered entities. Each separate health plan offered by the employer is a separate covered entity.

C. Transaction Standards

Any health plan that engages in the standard transactions, whether directly or through a third party, must be prepared to conduct those transactions electronically, using the standardized format and content set forth in the regulations. Most employer-sponsored health plans will probably rely on an insurer/HMO or a TPA for compliance with the electronic transactions requirement. Employers should check with their insurer, HMO, or TPA to verify they are on track to comply with the requirements by the deadline. Self-insured plans that are administered by the employer will need to take their own steps to assure readiness by the compliance date.

Enrollment transactions represent a special case. While the health plan is generally considered to be the party conducting the standard transactions, enrollment transactions may be viewed as being originated by the employer, rather than the employer-sponsored plan. And because the employer is not the covered entity, the enrollment information transmitted from the employer to its health plan is not subject to the Transaction Standards.[1]

---

[1] 65 Fed. Reg. 50317 and 50318.

D. Privacy Regulations

Employers offering self-insured group health plans will be the most directly affected and those health plans will be responsible for full compliance with the HIPAA regulations, even if they use a TPA for plan administration. Employers offering fully insured plans will be able to delegate many compliance functions to the insurer but the employer's group health plan will retain some responsibilities.

1. Self-Insured Health Plans

In general, a self-insured or self-funded group health plan sponsored by an employer must comply with <u>all</u> health plan requirements under the Privacy Regulations. In addition, the following are some special provisions that apply only to employer-sponsored health plans:

a. Limited Employer Access to PHI. Employers may not access any health plan PHI for non-plan purposes, and especially not for employment-related purposes.[2] For example, an employer may not reassign an employee to another job based on information from the health plan that the employee is being treated for alcoholism. An employer receives personal information about employees from a variety of sources, including directly from the employee. The concern of the Privacy Regulations, however, is information received from or through the employer's health plan.

b. Firewalls. Employers must establish a "firewall" between plan-related uses of PHI and general corporate or employment-related uses of PHI.[3] Employers who currently have the same individual or group of individuals handling all benefit plans plus human resource matters should consider separating these functions. In small organizations where having different staff members for these functions is not feasible, the employer should, at a minimum, establish policies and conduct training regarding the confidentiality of PHI and the need to restrict uses as well as disclosures.

TPAs contacting an employer will need to be careful about which staff members at the employer's offices they communicate with, so that PHI is communicated only to authorized personnel. Covered entities and business associates will need to carefully consider the appropriate avenues of communication.

Employment records are not PHI, even if they contain health information about an employee.[4] Employment records are not subject to this "firewall" requirement, but in fact will always be employer information rather than plan information. Employment records may include medical information needed for an employer to carry out its obligations under the Family and Medical Leave Act, Americans with Disabilities Act, and similar laws, as well as files or records related to occupational injury, disability insurance eligibility, sick leave requests and justifications, drug screening results, workplace medical surveillance, and fitness-for-duty tests of employees.[5]

c. Plan Document. The health plan's plan document must be amended to include a number of specific provisions relating to privacy. No disclosures from the health plan to the employer are permitted until the plan document is amended. The plan document must identify all permitted and required uses and disclosures of PHI by the employer for plan administra-

---

[2] 45 C.F.R. § 164.504(f)(3)(iv); 65 Fed. Reg. 82508.
[3] 45 C.F.R. § 164.504(f)(2)(iii); 65 Fed. Reg. 82508.
[4] 45 C.F.R. § 164.501.
[5] 67 Fed. Reg. 53192 (Aug. 14, 2002).

tion purposes. The plan document must state that the employer will not use PHI received from the plan for employment-related actions or decisions, or in connection with any of the employer's other health plans. The plan document must identify which employees or classes of employees of the plan sponsor, or other persons under control of the plan sponsor, are to be to be given access to PHI (e.g., a benefits clerk, a benefits committee, or claims appeal committee). In addition, the employer must ensure that there is adequate separation between the employer and the plan to protect the privacy of plan-held information.[6] A sample plan amendment is provided in Appendix B.

The following are some key provisions that apply to all health plans, but raise special issues in the context of an employer-sponsored health plans:

d. Consents and Authorizations. A health plan does not need an individual's consent or acknowledgement of its notice of privacy practices to use or disclose PHI for treatment, payment, or health care operations. These activities include claim payment, stop-loss claims, subrogation, evaluating plan performance, underwriting, auditing, and medical reviews. Disclosures to comply with workers' compensation laws also do not require consent.[7] Other uses and disclosures of information by the health plan require a written authorization from the individual. Examples of uses/disclosures that would require such authorization include any disclosures by the health plan to the plan sponsor for non-plan purposes or providing names of individuals covered by the medical plan to a long-term care insurer for marketing purposes. Employers should conduct an inventory of the plan's PHI uses and disclosures to determine which, if any, require such authorization.

e. Notice of Privacy Practices. The group health plan's notice of privacy practices must state that the health plan, or the health plan's insurer or HMO may disclose PHI to the employer, as plan sponsor, for plan administration functions.

f. Requests for Access and Amendments; Accounting for Disclosures. The health plan must establish a procedure for handling these requests. If most of the health plan PHI is held by a TPA, the TPA may perform these functions on behalf of the health plan. If so, these services should be made an obligation of the TPA under the administrative services contract, and appropriate policies and procedures should be developed. The ultimate responsibility for these functions remains with the health plan, however. The notice of privacy practices should explain whether individuals should contact the TPA or the employer with these requests.

g. Complaints. The health plan must establish a procedure to handle privacy complaints from individuals. The notice of privacy practices should explain whether individuals should contact the TPA or the employer with complaints.

h. Business Associate Agreements. A health plan will typically outsource some plan administration activities. Any outside entity that receives PHI from the plan in order to perform functions on behalf of the plan is a business associate of the health plan. Business associates may include, for example, TPAs, preferred provider organizations, utilization review companies, subrogation recovery firms, accounting firms, insurance brokers, consultants, and outside legal counsel. The plan must have the required business associate agreements in place with each such business associate. The business associate agreement provisions may be incorporated in another contract, such as an administrative services agreement with a TPA.

---

[6] 45 C.F.R. § 164.504(f)(2)(iii); 65 Fed. Reg. 82508.
[7] 45 C.F.R. § 164.512(l).

i. Administrative Requirements. The employer-sponsored health plan is also subject to the Privacy Regulations' administrative requirements. The plan must:

- Designate a privacy official;
- Document the plan's privacy policies and procedures;
- Conduct privacy training;
- Establish information security measures;
- Establish a system for reporting noncompliance; and
- Establish and enforce sanctions for policy violations.

2. Insured Health Plans

Employer-sponsored health plans that offer benefits through an insurance contract with a health insurance company or HMO (Insured Plans) are also covered entities under HIPAA. For Insured Plans, however, most of the compliance responsibilities discussed above will fall on the insurer or HMO, not on the employer or plan sponsor. For example, the insurer or HMO will typically handle compliance with regard to the individual's right to access and amend their records, and to obtain an accounting of disclosures. The policy behind this limited-compliance approach for the Insured Plan is that the insurance company or HMO will be providing these individual rights and privacy protections in its own role as a covered entity, and the incremental value of having the employer's Insured Plan duplicate these activities would not justify the additional burdens on the plan sponsor. The obligations of an Insured Plan with regard to HIPAA compliance are determined by the approach the plan takes to PHI.

a. The Hands-Off Approach. Insured Plans can reduce their privacy obligations if they take a "hands-off" approach to PHI. An employer-sponsored health plan is not subject to most Privacy Regulations requirements if it provides benefits solely through an insurance contract with an insurer or HMO. To qualify under this "hands-off" approach, the Insured Plan may not create or receive any PHI, except that it may receive from the insurer or HMO enrollment and disenrollment information and summary health information for the purpose of obtaining premium bids or modifying, amending, or terminating the plan.[8] With this "hands off" approach, the Insured Plan is exempted from most of the requirements under the Privacy Regulations.[9] These Insured Plans must still, however, limit employer access to PHI and the plan sponsor/employer may not use PHI for employment purposes. Furthermore, the Insured Plan cannot retaliate against or intimidate an employee exercising his or her rights under the Privacy Regulations or require that an employee waive his or her right to file a complaint with DHHS as a condition for eligibility or participation in the plan. If the Insured Plan shares any PHI with the plan sponsor (employer) other than enrollment/disenrollment

---

[8] For purposes of these provisions relating to disclosure of enrollment and disenrollment information from the health plan to the employer, the enrollment and disenrollment information may not include medical information about the individual above and beyond that which is required (or situationally required) by the HIPAA Transactions Standards. 67 Fed. Reg. 53208.

Summary health information is information that summarizes the claims history, expenses, or types of claims by individuals enrolled in the group health plan. To be considered summary health information, the identifiers listed under the safe harbor for de-identification in § 164.514(b)(2)(i) must be removed prior to disclosing the information to a plan sponsor, except that the data may be aggregated to the level of a 5-digit zip code. 45 C.F.R. § 164.504(a). Summary health information does not constitute de-identified information because there may be a reasonable basis to believe the information is identifiable to the plan sponsor, especially if the number of participants in the group health plan is small. 65 Fed. Reg. 82647.

[9] 45 C.F.R. §§ 164.504(f); 164.520(a)(2)(iii); 164.530(k).

information and summary health information, the plan document must be amended as described above.[10]

b. The Hands-On Approach. If the Insured Plan does create or receive PHI in addition to enrollment/disenrollment and summary health information, i.e., it takes a "hands-on" approach, it is generally subject to all of the Privacy Regulations requirements, including all of the administrative requirements discussed above, such as appointing a privacy official, documenting its policies and procedures, and providing training for its workforce. The Insured Plan's responsibilities with regard to the notice of privacy practices are reduced, however. The Insured Plan must prepare and maintain a notice of privacy practices and provide that notice upon request (to anyone), but is not required to distribute the notice to all plan participants.

All health plans, including all Insured Plans, must limit employer access to PHI as described above and may not use health plan PHI for employment purposes.

E. Security Regulations

In addition to the Privacy Regulations, employer-sponsored group health plans will be required to comply with the HIPAA Security Regulations, once finalized.

Application of the HIPAA Administrative Simplification Regulations to employers and plan sponsors is one of the most complex areas of HIPAA. Additional guidance from DHHS would be welcome in this regard.

---

[10] *See* 67 Fed. Reg. 53208.

APPENDIX A: SAMPLE BUSINESS ASSOCIATE CONTRACT

MODEL BUSINESS ASSOCIATE CONTRACT PROVISIONS[1]
[To be customized for the specific business relationship, with advice of legal counsel.]

I. **Definitions (alternative approaches)**

Catch-all definition:

Terms used, but not otherwise defined, in this Agreement shall have the same meaning as those terms in 45 C.F.R. §§ 160.103 and 164.501.

Examples of specific definitions:

(a) Business Associate. "Business Associate" shall mean [Insert Name of Business Associate].
(b) Covered Entity. "Covered Entity" shall mean [Insert Name of Covered Entity].
(c) Individual. "Individual" shall have the same meaning as the term "individual" in 45 C.F.R. § 164.501 and shall include a person who qualifies as a personal representative in accordance with 45 C.F.R. § 164.502(g).
(d) Privacy Rule. "Privacy Rule" shall mean the Standards for Privacy of Individually Identifiable Health Information at 45 C.F.R. Part 160 and Part 164, Subparts A and E.
(e) Protected Health Information. "Protected Health Information" shall have the same meaning as the term "protected health information" in 45 C.F.R. § 164.501, limited to the information created or received by Business Associate from or on behalf of Covered Entity.
(f) Required By Law. "Required By Law" shall have the same meaning as the term "required by law" in 45 C.F.R. § 164.501.
(g) Secretary. "Secretary" shall mean the Secretary of the Department of Health and Human Services or his or her designee.

II. **Obligations and Activities of Business Associate**

(a) Business Associate agrees to not use or further disclose Protected Health Information other than as permitted or required by the Agreement or as Required By Law. [Comment: Consider (1) prohibiting Business Associate from de-identifying PHI for Business Associate's own use, and (2) requiring the Business Associate to provide notice to the Covered Entity of disclosures made as "Required by Law."]
(b) Business Associate agrees to use appropriate safeguards to prevent use or disclosure of the Protected Health Information other than as provided for by this Agreement. [Comment: Consider providing more detail regarding the "appropriate safeguards" requirements, as appropriate for the particular services; for example, by requiring training of Business Associate's workforce or Business Associate discipline of its workforce for violations.]
(c) Business Associate agrees to mitigate, to the extent practicable, any harmful effect that is known to Business Associate of a use or disclosure of Protected Health Information by Business Associate in violation of the requirements of this Agreement. [This provision may be included if it is appropriate for the Covered Entity to pass on its duty to mitigate damages by a Business Associate.] [Comment: **This mitigation provision is not required.**]

---

[1] This model Business Associate agreement was proposed by DHHS on March 27, 2002. 67 Fed. Reg. 14809. The language contained in brackets are DHHS comments. The language in **bold** and brackets are the author's comments.

(d) Business Associate agrees to report to Covered Entity any use or disclosure of the Protected Health Information not provided for by this Agreement. [**Comment: Consider providing details about the mechanics and timing of this process.**]

(e) Business Associate agrees to ensure that any agent, including a subcontractor, to whom it provides Protected Health Information received from, or created or received by Business Associate on behalf of Covered Entity agrees to the same restrictions and conditions that apply through this Agreement to Business Associate with respect to such information.

(f) Business Associate agrees to provide access, at the request of Covered Entity, and in the time and manner designated by Covered Entity, to Protected Health Information in a Designated Record Set, to Covered Entity or, as directed by Covered Entity, to an Individual in order to meet the requirements under 45 C.F.R. § 164.524. [Not necessary if business associate does not have protected health information in a designated record set.] [**Comment: This DHHS comment is their first indication that a provision required by the regulation may be <u>omitted</u> from the Business Associate agreement under these circumstances.**]

(g) Business Associate agrees to make any amendment(s) to Protected Health Information in a Designated Record Set that the Covered Entity directs or agrees to pursuant to 45 C.F.R. § 164.526 at the request of Covered Entity or an Individual, and in the time and manner designated by Covered Entity. [Not necessary if business associate does not have protected health information in a designated record set.] [**Comment:** *See* **comment under (f).**]

(h) Business Associate agrees to make internal practices, books, and records relating to the use and disclosure of Protected Health Information received from, or created or received by Business Associate on behalf of, Covered Entity available to the Covered Entity, or at the request of the Covered Entity to the Secretary, in a time and manner designated by the Covered Entity or the Secretary, for purposes of the Secretary determining Covered Entity's compliance with the Privacy Rule.

(i) Business Associate agrees to document such disclosures of Protected Health Information and information related to such disclosures as would be required for Covered Entity to respond to a request by an Individual for an accounting of disclosures of Protected Health Information in accordance with 45 C.F.R. § 164.528.

(j) Business Associate agrees to provide to Covered Entity or an Individual, in time and manner designated by Covered Entity, information collected in accordance with Section [Insert Section Number in Contract Where Provision Appears] of this Agreement, to permit Covered Entity to respond to a request by an Individual for an accounting of disclosures of Protected Health Information in accordance with 45 C.F.R. § 164.528.

III. <u>General Use and Disclosure Provisions [(alternative approaches)]</u>

<u>[Specify purposes:</u>]

Except as otherwise limited in this Agreement, Business Associate may use or disclose Protected Health Information on behalf of, or to provide services to, Covered Entity for the following purposes, if such use or disclosure of Protected Health Information would not violate the Privacy Rule if done by Covered Entity:

[List purposes].

<u>[Refer to underlying services agreement</u>:]

Except as otherwise limited in this Agreement, Business Associate may use or disclose Protected Health Information to perform functions, activities, or services for, or on behalf of,

Covered Entity as specified in [Insert Name of Services Agreement], provided that such use or disclosure would not violate the Privacy Rule if done by Covered Entity.

IV. **Specific Use and Disclosure Provisions [only necessary if parties wish to allow Business Associate to engage in such activities]**

(a) Except as otherwise limited in this Agreement, Business Associate may use Protected Health Information for the proper management and administration of the Business Associate or to carry out the legal responsibilities of the Business Associate.

(b) Except as otherwise limited in this Agreement, Business Associate may disclose Protected Health Information for the proper management and administration of the Business Associate, provided that disclosures are required by law, or Business Associate obtains reasonable assurances from the person to whom the information is disclosed that it will remain confidential and used or further disclosed only as required by law or for the purpose for which it was disclosed to the person, and the person notifies the Business Associate of any instances of which it is aware in which the confidentiality of the information has been breached.

(c) Except as otherwise limited in this Agreement, Business Associate may use Protected Health Information to provide Data Aggregation services to Covered Entity as permitted by 42 C.F.R. § 164.504(e)(2)(i)(B). [**Comment: Will not apply to most agreements, but should be included if data aggregation services are part of the agreement.**]

V. **Provisions for Covered Entity To Inform Business Associate of Privacy Practices and Restrictions [provisions dependent on business arrangement]**

[**Comment: The following three provisions are not required but generally represent advisable practices.**]

(a) Covered Entity shall provide Business Associate with the notice of privacy practices that Covered Entity produces in accordance with 45 C.F.R. § 164.520, as well as any changes to such notice.

(b) Covered Entity shall provide Business Associate with any changes in, or revocation of, permission by Individual to use or disclose Protected Health Information, if such changes affect Business Associate's permitted or required uses and disclosures.

(c) Covered Entity shall notify Business Associate of any restriction to the use or disclosure of Protected Health Information that Covered Entity has agreed to in accordance with 45 C.F.R. § 164.522.

VI. **Permissible Requests by Covered Entity**

Covered Entity shall not request Business Associate to use or disclose Protected Health Information in any manner that would not be permissible under the Privacy Rule if done by Covered Entity. [Include an exception if the Business Associate will use or disclose protected health information for, and the contract includes provisions for, data aggregation or management and administrative activities of Business Associate.]

VII. **Term and Termination**

(a) Term. The Term of this Agreement shall be effective as of [Insert Effective Date], and shall terminate when all of the Protected Health Information provided by Covered Entity to Business Associate, or created or received by Business Associate on behalf of Covered Entity, is destroyed or returned to Covered Entity, or, if it is infeasible to return or destroy Protected Health Information, protections are extended to such information, in accordance with the termination provisions in this Section. [**Comment: Consider establishing timetable for return or destruction, and, if applicable, specify manner of destruction and provision of evidence of destruction.**]

(b) <u>Termination for Cause</u>. Upon Covered Entity's knowledge of a material breach by Business Associate, Covered Entity shall provide an opportunity for Business Associate to cure the breach or end the violation and terminate this Agreement [and the _____ Agreement/ sections ___ of the _____ Agreement] if Business Associate does not cure the breach or end the violation within the time specified by Covered Entity, or immediately terminate this Agreement [and the _____ Agreement/ sections ___ of the _____ Agreement] if Business Associate has breached a material term of this Agreement and cure is not possible. [Bracketed language in this provision may be necessary if there is an underlying services agreement. Also, opportunity to cure is permitted, but not required by the Privacy Rule.]

[**Comment: These termination provisions should be drafted in coordination with the termination provisions relative to the underlying services agreement. Also, immediate termination may be warranted in some circumstances.**]

(c) <u>Effect of Termination</u>.
  (1) Except as provided in paragraph (2) of this section, upon termination of this Agreement, for any reason, Business Associate shall return or destroy all Protected Health Information received from Covered Entity, or created or received by Business Associate on behalf of Covered Entity. This provision shall apply to Protected Health Information that is in the possession of subcontractors or agents of Business Associate. Business Associate shall retain no copies of the Protected Health Information.
  (2) In the event that Business Associate determines that returning or destroying the Protected Health Information is infeasible, Business Associate shall provide to Covered Entity notification of the conditions that make return or destruction infeasible. Upon mutual agreement of the Parties that return or destruction of Protected Health Information is infeasible, Business Associate shall extend the protections of this Agreement to such Protected Health Information and limit further uses and disclosures of such Protected Health Information to those purposes that make the return or destruction infeasible, for so long as Business Associate maintains such Protected Health Information.

VIII. Miscellaneous

(a) <u>Regulatory References</u>. A reference in this Agreement to a section in the Privacy Rule means the section as in effect or as amended, and for which compliance is required.
(b) <u>Amendment</u>. The Parties agree to take such action as is necessary to amend this Agreement from time to time as is necessary for Covered Entity to comply with the requirements of the Privacy Rule and the Health Insurance Portability and Accountability Act, Public Law 104-191.
(c) <u>Survival</u>. The respective rights and obligations of Business Associate under Section [Insert Section Number Related to "Effect of Termination"] of this Agreement shall survive the termination of this Agreement.
(d) <u>Interpretation</u>. Any ambiguity in this Agreement shall be resolved in favor of a meaning that permits Covered Entity to comply with the Privacy Rule. [Comment: Not a required provision, but recommended.]

[Comment: Additional provisions to consider (in consultation with legal counsel).]

a. Limitation of liability
b. Insurance
c. Survival
d. Access controls
e. Confidentiality (referencing state and other federal law)
f. Chain of trust (see HIPAA Security Standards)
g. Remedies
h. Monitoring compliance
i. Amending the agreement
j. Third party beneficiaries
k. Cooperation to achieve compliance
l. Ownership of information
m. Subcontractor approval]

APPENDIX B: SAMPLE PLAN DOCUMENT AMENDMENT

CONFIDENTIALITY OF PLAN INFORMATION
[To be customized for the specific circumstances, with advice of legal counsel.][1]

Plan Sponsor Certification: These provisions of the Plan are intended by the Plan and Plan Sponsor to comply with the provisions of the Health Insurance Portability and Accountability Act of 1996 ("HIPAA") privacy regulations at 45 C.F.R. § 164.504(f). [Assumes Plan (group health plan) and Plan Sponsor are defined in the plan document.]

Uses and Disclosures of Individually Identifiable Health Information: The Plan Sponsor may use and disclose protected health information, as defined in 45 C.F.R. § 164.501, which it receives from the Plan, only as follows:

[Describe Plan Sponsor's uses and disclosures of PHI for plan administration purposes.]

The Plan Sponsor shall not use or further disclose protected health information other than as permitted or required by the plan documents or as required by law.

Agents of Plan Sponsor: The Plan Sponsor shall ensure that any agents or subcontractors to whom the Plan Sponsor provides protected health information agree to the same restrictions and conditions that apply to the Plan Sponsor with respect to such information.

Prohibited Uses and Disclosures: The Plan Sponsor shall not use or disclose protected health information received from the Plan for employment-related actions and decisions. The Plan Sponsor shall not use or disclose protected health information received from the Plan in connection with any other benefit or employee benefit plan of the Plan Sponsor.

Reporting: If the Plan Sponsor becomes aware of any use or disclosure of protected health information that is inconsistent with the uses and disclosures provided for herein, the Plan Sponsor shall report it to the Plan.

Individual Rights: The Plan Sponsor shall (A) make available protected health information to individuals in accordance with the access rights in 45 C.F.R. § 164.524; (B) make protected health information available for amendment and incorporate any amendments in accordance with 45 C.F.R. § 164.526; (C) make available the information required to provide an accounting of disclosures in accordance with 45 C.F.R. § 164.528.

HHS Audits: The Plan Sponsor shall make its internal practices, books, and records relating to the use and disclosure of protected health information received from the Plan available to the Secretary of Health & Human Services for purposes of determining the Plan's compliance with the HIPAA privacy regulations.

Information Retention: If feasible, the Plan Sponsor shall return or destroy all protected health information received from the Plan that the Plan Sponsor still maintains in any form and retain no copies of such information when no longer needed for the purpose for which the disclosure was made. If such return or destruction is not feasible, the Plan Sponsor shall limit further uses and disclosures to those purposes that make the return or destruction of the information infeasible.

Separation: The Plan and Plan Sponsor shall ensure that adequate separation is established between the Plan and Plan Sponsor. The [**Identify employees or classes of employees—Note: Must include any employee or person who receives protected health information relating to (a) payment under the Plan, (b) health care operations of the Plan, or (c) other matters pertaining to the Plan in ordinary course of business.**] may have access to

---

[1] The language in **bold** and brackets are the author's comments.

protected health information disclosed by the Plan. Such persons' access to and use of protected health information shall be limited to the Plan administration functions that the Plan Sponsor performs for the Plan. Noncompliance by such persons with the requirements of this paragraph may result in **[Describe sanctions]**.

APPENDIX C: STATE-BY-STATE GUIDE TO MEDICAL PRIVACY STATUTES

Prepared by Aureliano Sanchez-Arango, J.D.

State	Health Care Privacy Statute/Provisions	Specific Disclosure Rules
ALABAMA	No general prohibition on disclosure of confidential medical information. Mental health patients have right of confidentiality of all information in mental health, medical, and financial records. Communications between mental health caregivers granted same status as attorney–client communications [Ala. Code §§ 34-26-2, 34-8A-21, and 15-23-42]. An HMO may also claim privilege available to provider [Ala. Code § 27-21A-25]. No physician–patient privilege [Ala. Code §§ 22-56-4 and 22-56-10]. Health plans may not use genetic testing results to set premiums or require genetic testing [Ala. Code § 27-53-2].	• Apply to HMOs and utilization review agents [Ala. Code 27-3A-5(c)(7)] with exceptions [Ala. Code § 27-21A-25]. • Apply to specific medical conditions including information contained in reports submitted to state-wide cancer registry, sexually transmitted diseases, and mandatory tuberculosis reports submitted to health agencies [Ala. Code §§ 22-13-33, 22-13-34, §§ 22-11A-14 and 22-11A-22, and §§ 22-11A-9].

continues

State	Health Care Privacy Statute/Provisions	Specific Disclosure Rules
ALASKA	No general prohibition on disclosure of confidential medical information. Mental health records are confidential [Alaska Stat. § 47.30.845], information maintained by a pharmacist in a patient record is confidential [Alaska Stat. § 8.80.315], and numerous health care provider–patient privileges exist [Alaska R. Evid. 504 and Alaska Stat. § 9.25.400]. Electronic medical records are allowed as long as the physical security of the records is protected from access by unauthorized persons [Alaska Stat. § 18.23.100].	• HMOs may not disclose medical information about enrollees or applicants without patient's consent, with exceptions for purposes of HMO legislation and court orders [Alaska Stat. 21.86.280]. • Data on birth defects, cancer, and infectious diseases that must be reported to the department of health is confidential [Alaska Stat. § 18.05.042]. • Medical records of patient who has been treated by emergency medical services (EMS) provider may be disclosed to that provider for purposes of evaluating performance of EMS personnel [Alaska Stat. 18.08.087].

State	Health Care Privacy Statute/Provisions	Specific Disclosure Rules
ARIZONA	Medical records and the information they contain are confidential and privileged [Ariz. Rev. Stat. § 12-2292]. Privilege applies to physicians, dentists, hospitals, pharmacists, psychologists, health care service organizations, and others [Ariz. Rev. Stat. § 12-2291]. Numerous health care provider–patient privileges exist [Ariz. Rev. Stat. §§ 12-2235, 32-2085, and 32-3283]. Mental health records are confidential, with certain excep-tions [Ariz. Rev. Sat. § 36-509]. Genetic test results are confidential [Ariz. Rev. Stat. § 20-448.02].	• Providers may disclose a patient's medical information without the patient's consent to: other current or previous health care providers for purposes of diagnosing or treating the patient; ambulance attendants providing care or transferring the patient; accrediting agencies; providers, for utilization review or peer review; billing, claims management or medical data processing entities; the provider's legal representative for securing legal advice; a deceased patient's administrator; third-party payors, with written authorization; the patient's health care decision maker at the time of the patient's death [Ariz. Rev. Stat. § 12-2294]. • Insurance entities may disclose medical record information without the person's written authorization to prevent fraud or to verify insurance coverage; to conduct business when disclosure is reasonably necessary; to law enforcement agencies in situations involving fraud; under subpoena or court order; for marketing purposes, with certain restrictions [Ariz. Rev. Stat. § 20-2113]. • Mental health information may be disclosed to physicians and other providers treating or caring for the patient, individuals with consent of the patient, persons legally representing the patient, persons doing research or maintaining health statistics, in the case of prisoners, to the department of corrections, law enforcement to secure the return of patients absent without authorization, family members participating in the patient's care, health care professional licensing agencies investigating malpractice claims; or pursuant to a court order [Ariz. Rev. Stat. § 36-509]. • Cancer, birth defects, and other chronic diseases must be reported to the Department of Health Services to be used for certain limited purposes [Ariz. Rev. Stat. § 36-133].

continues

State	Health Care Privacy Statute/Provisions	Specific Disclosure Rules
ARKANSAS	No general prohibition on disclosure of confidential medical information. Numerous health care provider-patient privileges exist [Ark. Rules of Evidence 503 (physician and psychotherapist-patient); Ark. Code Ann. §§ 17-27-311 (family therapist-client), 17-103-107 (social worker-client), and 17-97-105 (psychologist-patient)].	• HMOs may not disclose an enrollee's or applicant's medical information except as necessary to carry out the purposes of the HMO statute, with the person's express consent, pursuant to statute or court order, or a claim between the person and the HMO [Ark. Code Ann. § 23-76-129]. • State Hospital records and information compiled for purposes of mental health research and containing patient-identifying information may be used only for that purpose and may not be otherwise disclosed [Ark. Code Ann. § 20-46-104]. • Utilization review agents may not disclose confidential medical information obtained during UR activities without appropriate procedures for protecting the patient's confidentiality [Ark. Code Ann. § 20-9-913]. • Certain conditions must be reported to the state but must be treated as confidential by the facility, registry, or agency to whom reported, including actual or suspected cases of abuse or neglect of impaired adults [Ark. Code Ann. § 5-28-213], cancer [§ 20-15-203], HIV/AIDS [§ 20-15-904], conditions reviewed for morbidity and mortality research [§ 20-9-304], trauma [§ 20-13-806], and venereal diseases [§ 20-16-504]. Employers and insurers are prohibited from requiring genetic testing or using results of genetic tests as a condition of employment or insurance [Ark. Code Ann. §§ 11-5-403, 23-66-320].

State	Health Care Privacy Statute/Provisions	Specific Disclosure Rules
CALIFORNIA	The Confidentiality of Medical Information Act (CMIA) requires health care providers and employers to obtain written consent from patients before disclosing identifiable information, with numerous exceptions [Cal. Civ. Code § 56.10 exceptions applying to coroner's office added to this section as of Jan. 1, 2003]. Mental health information and records are confidential [Cal. Welf. & Inst. Code §§ 5328 (as amended to include exceptions for report of elder and dependent adult abuse effective Jan. 1, 2003) and 5540]. Privileges are recognized with respect to patients and their physicians, psychotherapists, psychologists, social workers, nurses, and sexual assault or domestic abuse counselors [Cal. Evid. Code §§ 990 through 1037.7].	• Patient authorization for release of medical information is not required for disclosures related to the diagnosis, treatment, billing, emergencies, tissue transplants, licensing and accreditation, utilization review and quality assurance activities, pursuant to subpoenas or court orders, and other specified situations [Cal. Civ. Code § 56.10 (exceptions applying to coroner's office added to this section as of Jan. 1, 2003)]. • Insurers need not obtain written authorization from patients before disclosing personal information to verify coverage or benefits, to inform a person of a medical problem, to detect fraud, or for marketing purposes, as long as no medical record or information about a person's character, personal habits, or reputation is disclosed subject to an opt-out provision [Cal. Ins. Code § 791.13]. • Various conditions must be reported to the state but must be treated as confidential by the agency, registry, or program that receives the report. Conditions include birth defects [Cal. Health & Safety Code § 103850], cancer [Cal. Health & Safety Code § 103885], and HIV/AIDS [Cal. Health & Safety Code §§ 120975 to 21020].

continues

State	Health Care Privacy Statute/Provisions	Specific Disclosure Rules
COLORADO	No general prohibition on disclosure of confidential medical information. Restrictions on disclosure are found in statutes governing specific entities or conditions: health care coverage cooperatives [Colo. Rev. Stat. Ann. § 6-18-103]; psychologists, social workers and counselors [Colo. Rev. Stat. Ann. §§ 12-43-201 and 12-43-218]; and HMOs [Colo. Rev. Stat. § 10-16-423]. Records and information regarding mental illness are confidential and privileged [Colo. Rev. Stat. Ann. § 27-10-120]. Health care provider–patient privileges apply to physicians, surgeons, and registered nurses, and to psychologists, psychotherapists, social workers, professional counselors, and marriage and family therapists [Colo. Rev. Stat. Ann. § 13-90-107].	• HMOs may disclose medical information as necessary to carry out the statutory provisions regarding HMOs, pursuant to statute or court order for production of evidence, or where there is a claim or litigation between a person and the HMO [Colo. Rev. Stat. Ann. § 10-16-423]. • Disclosure of genetic testing information without patient consent is allowed for diagnosis, treatment, or therapy and for scientific research if the test subject's identity is not released to a third party [Colo. Rev. Stat. Ann. § 10-3-1104.7]. • Health care professionals must report incidents of cancer, venereal and other communicable diseases, and cases of AIDS/HIV to health authorities, but such reports are strictly confidential and may not be released, shared with any agency or institution, or made public upon subpoena, discovery proceedings, or otherwise, except in limited circumstance [Colo. Rev. Stat. Ann. §§ 25-1-107, 25-1-122, 25-4-402, 25-4-1404].

State	Health Care Privacy Statute/Provisions	Specific Disclosure Rules
CONNECTICUT	No general prohibition on disclosure of confidential medical information. Specific prohibitions against disclosure apply to employers [Conn. Gen. Stat. § 31-128f], insurance entities, including HMOs [Conn. Gen. Stat. §§ 38a-989 (technical amendments only, effective Oct. 1, 2002), 38a-976 (technical amendments only, effective Sept. 1, 2002), 38a-977], and pharmacists [Conn. Gen. Stat. § 20-626]. Health care provider-patient privileges exist for physicians, psychologists, psychiatrists, sexual assault counselors, and marital and family therapists [Conn. Gen. Stat. § 52-146 *et seq.*].	• Insurers, including HMOs, can disclose information without a person's authorization in order to verify insurance coverage benefits; to conduct business when disclosure is necessary; to law enforcement agencies, to prevent or prosecute fraud; and in response to a court order or subpoena [Conn. Gen. Stat. § 38a-988(k)]. • Records of treatment of a patient's mental condition may be disclosed without the patient's consent to others involved in the patient's diagnosis or treatment; when there is a substantial risk of imminent physical injury by the patient to himself or herself or others; to place the patient in a mental health facility; and in other situations [Conn. Gen. Stat. § 52-146f]. • Special disclosure rules apply to information obtained in connection with studies of morbidity and mortality [Conn. Gen. Stat. § 19a-25]; records of conception by artificial insemination [Conn. Gen. Stat. § 45a-773]; and HIV-related information [Conn. Gen. Stat. § 19a-583].

continues

State	Health Care Privacy Statute/Provisions	Specific Disclosure Rules
DELAWARE	No general statute protecting confidential medical information. Health care provider-patient privileges extended to physicians and psychotherapists (Del. Uniform Rules of Evidence, Rule 503], mental health counselors [Del. Code Ann. tit. 24, § 3019], and clinical social workers [Del. Code Ann. tit. 24, § 3913]. Mental health records are confidential, with certain exceptions [Del. Code Ann. tit. 16, § 5161]. Genetic information is confidential, with certain exceptions [Del. Code Ann. tit. 16, §§ 1220, 1221, 1222]. New comprehensive statute restricts government use of protected health information to legitimate public health purposes, restricts its disclosure, and requires the information be expunged when its use no longer furthers the public health purpose [Del. Code Ann. tit. 16, §§ 1230-1232, effective July 3, 2002].	• Managed care organizations (MCOs) may not disclose information about an enrollee's or applicant's diagnosis or treatment without the person's consent, except as required by statute, pursuant to court order, or in the case of a claim or litigation between the person and the MCO [Del. Code Ann. tit. 16, § 9113]. • Clinical social workers may disclose information obtained from a client without written consent in cases of threatened imminent violence, suspected child abuse, or if the person brings charges against the social worker [Del. Code Ann. tit. 24 § 2913]. • HIV test results may be disclosed without the subject's written consent to a health facility that procures, processes, or distributes blood [Del. Code Ann. tit. 16, § 1203]. Insurers are subject to specific laws governing HIV-related information [see Del. Code Ann. tit. 18, §§ 7404-7405]. • Hospitals and nursing homes must submit forms for all inpatient discharges to the state's health information data base, which is confidential [Del. Code Ann. tit. 16, § 2001]. • Cancer cases must be reported to a state registry that may exchange information with cancer control agencies, preventing patients' confidentiality [Del. Code Ann. tit. 16, § 3202, § 3205].

State	Health Care Privacy Statute/Provisions	Specific Disclosure Rules
DISTRICT OF COLUMBIA	No general prohibition on disclosure of medical information. Specific provisions against disclosure apply to certain entities [D.C. Code Ann. § 31-3426 (HMOs)] or medical conditions [D.C. Code Ann. § 31-1606 (AIDS testing)]. Disclosures of mental health information are prohibited [D.C. Code Ann. § 7-1201.01 *et seq.*]. Health care provider–patient privileges exist for physicians and mental health professionals [D.C. Code Ann. §§ 14-307, 7-1201.01 *et seq.*].	• HMOs may disclose medical information without consent to carry out the laws governing HMOs; where there is a claim or litigation between a person and the HMO; as needed to conduct business; and pursuant to statute or court order [D.C. Code Ann. § 31-3426]. • The amount and type of mental health information a provider may disclose to a third-party payor is limited, regardless of a valid authorization to disclose [D.C. Code Ann. § 7-1202.07]. • The amount and type of mental health information a provider may disclose to a third-party payor is limited, regardless of a valid authorization to disclose [D.C. Code Ann. § 7-1202.07]. Such information may also be disclosed: as necessary to facilitate treatment; as required by law; in an emergency to a person's spouse, parent, guardian, police officer, or an intended victim; for scientific research or management or financial audits; and in certain court proceedings [D.C. Code Ann. §§ 7-1203.01 through 7-1203.06, 7-1204.01 through 7-1204.05]. • Mandatory cancer and communicable disease reports may be used only for statistical and public health purposes, and identifying information may be disclosed without written permission or a court order only if essential to protect the physical health of others [D.C. Code Ann. §§ 7-131, 7-302, 7-1605].

continues

State	Health Care Privacy Statute/Provisions	Specific Disclosure Rules
FLORIDA	Patients have a general right to privacy in health care [Fla. Stat. Ann. 381.026]. A patient's records are confidential and may not be disclosed without written consent, nor may his or her medical condition be discussed with anyone other than the patient, his or her representative, or other providers involved in his or her care and treatment, with certain exceptions [Fla. Stat. Ann. § 456.057]. There are numerous laws protecting the confidentiality of medical information held by various entities [e.g., Fla. Stat. Ann. § 400.022 (nursing homes)] and government agencies [e.g., Fla. Stat. Ann. § 408.061 (Agency for Health Care Administration)]. Provider-patient privileges exist for psychotherapists and psychiatrists [Fla. Stat. Ann. §§ 90.503, 456-059 and 490.147].	• Health care providers may furnish records without patient consent as provided by law; pursuant to subpoena; for statistical or scientific research, if the patient's identity is protected. Providers may disclose medical information only to other providers involved in the patient's care; pursuant to subpoena and to the Health Department [Fla. Stat. Ann. § 456.057], and to research groups, and government agencies conducting morbidity and mortality studies [Fla. Stat. Ann. § 405.01]. • Insurers and HMOs may not disclose information regarding psychotherapeutic services, and such medical records are not subject to audit by the Insurance Department, but may be subpoenaed [Fla. Stat. Ann. §§ 627.4195, 641.59, 641.27, 636.039]. • Providers and facilities must maintain a record of all disclosures to a third party, including the purpose of the disclosure request, and keep it in the medical record [Fla. Stat. Ann. §§ 455.67]. • Hospitals may disclose patient records without patient consent to facility personnel and physicians in connection with the patient's treatment; for administrative, risk management and quality assurance or cost containment purposes; pursuant to subpoena; to organ procurement entities and tissue and eye banks; and to state agencies and entities as required by law [Fla. Stat. Ann. § 395.3025]. • Other specific disclosure rules apply to HIV testing [Fla. Stat. Ann. §§ 381.004, 456.061, 627,429, and 641.3007]; reportable and sexually transmitted diseases [Fla. Stat. Ann. §§ 381.0031, 119.07, and 384.29]; and substance abuse [Fla. Stat. Ann. § 397.501].

State	Health Care Privacy Statute/Provisions	Specific Disclosure Rules
GEORGIA	No general prohibition on disclosure of confidential medical information. Specific prohibitions against disclosure apply to various entities and medical conditions, e.g., HMOs and insurance entities [Ga. Code §§ 33-21-23 and 33-39-14], information provided to research groups [Ga. Code § 31-7-6], and genetic testing [Ga. Code § 33-54-3]. There is no statutory physician-patient privilege, but there is a privilege extended to patients of psychiatrists, psychologists, clinical social workers, and marriage counselors. [Ga. Code § 24-9-21]	• HMOs may disclose enrollee or applicant medical information as necessary to carry out the law governing HMOs, pursuant to court order or statute, or in the event of claim or litigation by the person against the HMO [Ga. Code § 33-21-23]. • An insurance entity may disclose medical information without authorization to verify coverage benefits to a provider; as necessary to conduct the insurer's business; to law enforcement agencies, to prevent or prosecute fraud; pursuant to subpoena or search warrant [Ga. Code § 33-39-14]. • Physicians, pharmacists, hospitals, and health care facilities are required to release patient medical information to the Department of Human Resources as necessary for public health programs; where authorized or required by law; and pursuant to court order or subpoena [Ga. Code § 24-9-40]. • Specific disclosure rules apply to the records of patients in mental facilities [Ga. Code § 37-3-166], and to HIV status [Ga. Code § 24-9-47].

continues

State	Health Care Privacy Statute/Provisions	Specific Disclosure Rules
HAWAII	Hawaii no longer has a general, comprehensive law prohibiting disclosure of private medical information. There are numerous laws concerning disclosure of medical information possessed by various entities [Haw. Rev. Stat. §§ 432D-21 (HMOs), 432E-10 (Managed Care Plans), 328-16 (Practitioners and Pharmacists), 334B-5 (Utilization Review Agents)]. State agencies are covered under the Uniform Information Practices Act [Haw. Rev. Stat. § 92F-1 *et seq.*]. There are a number of health provider–patient privileges, applying to physicians, psychologists, and other counselors—subject to newly enacted exceptions for certain proceedings [Haw. Rev. Stat. Ann. § 626-1, Haw. R. of Evid. 504, 504.1, 505.5].	• Specific disclosure rules apply to HIV/AIDS status [Haw. Rev. Stat. Ann. § 325-101], cancer [Haw. Rev. Stat. Ann. § 324-22], communicable diseases [Haw. Rev. Stat. Ann. § 325-4], and mental health and mental retardation [Haw. Rev. Stat. Ann. §§ 324-12 and 324-13]. Insurers and HMOs may not require or disclose genetic information, subject to exceptions [Haw. Rev. Stat. §§ 431:10A-101, 431:10A-118, 432D-26].

State	Health Care Privacy Statute/Provisions	Specific Disclosure Rules
IDAHO	No general prohibition on disclosure of medical information. Privacy protections are contained in statutes governing specific medical conditions or entities. Records of persons in mental facilities or assisted-living facilities are confidential [Idaho Code §§ 39-3315 and 39-3316]. A number of health care provider-patient privileges exist [Idaho Code §§ 9-203(4) (physician-patient); 54-2314 (psychologist-client); and 54-3410 (professional counselor-client)].	• Alcohol and drug treatment facilities may make records available for research into treatment of substance abuse; researchers may not publish their information in a manner that identifies any patient [Idaho Code § 39-308]. • Cancer registry information may be exchanged with other states' registries, federal cancer control programs or health researchers [Idaho Code § 57-1706]. • Physicians and nursing homes must report suspected cases of abuse or neglect of vulnerable adults [Idaho Code § 39-5303]. • Specific disclosure rules apply to persons being treated for HIV/AIDS and venereal diseases [Idaho Code §§ 39-602 through 399-606].

continues

State	Health Care Privacy Statute/Provisions	Specific Disclosure Rules
ILLINOIS	A patient's right to privacy and confidentiality in health care extends to information in the possession of physicians, medical providers, health services corporations, and insurers, including HMOs. The nature or details of services provided to a patient cannot be disclosed without written authorization [410 Ill. Comp. Stat. 50/3(d)]. A health care provider-patient privilege extends to a patient and his or her physician, surgeon, psychologist, nurse, mental health worker, therapist, and others, with certain exceptions [735 Ill. Comp. Stat. 5/8-802].	• Providers may disclose medical information without authorization to persons directly involved in treating the patient or processing payment for treatment; persons performing peer review or quality assurance functions; authorities in suspected child abuse or neglect cases, or incidences of sexually transmitted disease; or as otherwise required by law [410 Ill. Comp. Stat. 50/3(d)]. • Insurers and HMOs may disclose medical record information without authorization; to a medical professional to verify insurance benefits; to agents when necessary to conduct business; to law enforcement agencies, to prevent or prosecute fraud; and pursuant to search warrant or subpoena [215 Ill. Comp. Stat. 5/1014]. • Other specific disclosure rules apply to genetic testing [410 Ill. Comp. Stat. 513/15 and 513/30]; HIV/AIDS test results [410 Ill. Comp. 305/9]; mental health and developmental disabilities [740 Ill. Comp. Stat. 110/3, 110/5 through 110/12.2]; and sexually transmitted diseases [410 Ill. Comp. Stat. 325/8].

State	Health Care Privacy Statute/Provisions	Specific Disclosure Rules
INDIANA	No general prohibition on disclosure of confidential medical information. A number of health care provider-patient privileges exist: physician-patient [Ind. Code § 34-36-3-1]; psychologist-client [Ind. Code § 25-33-1-17]; social worker-client [Ind. Code § 25-23, 6-6-1]; victim counselor-client [Ind. Code § 35-37-6-9].	• Health care providers are the owners of a patient's original health record and may use it without patient consent for legitimate business purposes, including submission of claims for payment from third parties, collection of accounts, litigation defense, quality assurance and peer review, and scientific, statistical and educational purposes [Ind. Code § 16-39-5-3]. • HMOs may access an enrollee's treatment records and other medical information during the time the person is covered by the HMO, and may disclose information as necessary to carry out the law governing HMOs, pursuant to statute or court order, or for litigation defense [Ind. Code § 27-13-31-1]. • Hospital medical staff committees may access patient records for research, to gather statistics concerning prevention and treatment of diseases, and to reduce morbidity and mortality, but may not reveal patients' identity [Ind. Code § 16-39-6-1]. • Other specific disclosure rules apply to pharmacists [Ind. Code § 25-26-13-15]; the state cancer registry [Ind. Code §§ 16-39-2-1 through 16-38-2-7]; birth problems registry [Ind. Code §§ 16-38-4-1, 16-38-4-10, 16-38-4-11]; and communicable disease reporting [Ind. Code §§ 16-41-2-1 and 16-41-8-1].

continues

State	Health Care Privacy Statute/Provisions	Specific Disclosure Rules
IOWA	Hospital records, medical records, and professional counselor records of the diagnosis, care, or treatment of a patient are confidential [Iowa Code § 22.7]. A health care provider-patient privilege exists that extends to physicians, counselors, surgeons, physician's assistants, advanced registered nurse practitioners, mental health professionals, and their patients [Iowa Code § 622.10].	• Apply to third-party payors (such as insurers) or peer review organizations with respect to mental health information [Iowa Code § 228.7]. • Apply to providers of mental health services [Iowa Code §§ 228.2 through 228.8]. • Apply to specific medical conditions including brain injury reports to the public health department [Iowa Code § 135.22]; communicable diseases [Iowa Code §§ 22.7(16) and 139A.3]; HIV status [Iowa Code §§ 141A.5 and 141A.11]; and birth defects [Iowa Code § 136A.6].

State	Health Care Privacy Statute/Provisions	Specific Disclosure Rules
KANSAS	No general prohibition on disclosure of confidential medical information. Privacy is addressed in statutes governing specific entities, such as HMOs [Kan. Stat. Ann. § 40-3226(a)], or medical conditions, such as sickle cell anemia [Kan. Stat. Ann. § 65-1, 106]. Numerous health care provider–patient privileges exist [Kan. Stat. Ann. §§ 60-427 (physician-patient); 65-1654 (pharmacist-patient); 65-5601 and 65-5602 (mental health treatment personnel-patient); 65-5810 (professional counselor-client); 74-5323 and 74-5372 (psychologist-patient)].	• HMOs may disclose enrollee or applicant medical information as necessary to carry out the law governing HMOs, or as otherwise provided by law [Kan. Stat. Ann. § 40-3226(a)]. • Specific disclosure rules apply to utilization review organizations [Kan. Stat. Ann. §§ 40-22a09 and 40-22a10]. • Specific disclosure rules apply to alcohol and substance abuse treatment records [Kan. Stat. Ann. § 59-29b79]; mental health patients [Kan. Stat. Ann. §§ 65-5601 through 65-5603]; HIV/AIDS status [Kan. Stat. Ann. § 65-6002]; and reporting of contagious diseases [Kan. Stat. Ann. §§ 65-118 and 65-119].

continues

State	Health Care Privacy Statute/Provisions	Specific Disclosure Rules
KENTUCKY	No general prohibition on disclosure of medical information. Privacy is addressed in statutes, which govern specific entities or medical condi-tions. Records of patients in state mental facilities are confidential, with certain exceptions [Ky. Rev. Stat. Ann. § 210.235]. No physician-patient privilege exists, but there are numerous mental health care provider-patient privileges [Ky. Rules of evidence 506 and 507 (counselor-client and psychotherapist-patient)]. No privilege exists for involuntarily hospitalized mental patients.	• Private utilization review agents may disclose or publish individual medical records or information if there are appropriate procedures to protect the patient's confidentiality [Ky. Rev. Stat. Ann. § 311.139]. • Specific disclosure rules apply to reporting of cancer cases [Ky. Rev. Stat. Ann. § 214.556]; HIV test results [Ky. Rev. Stat. Ann. § 214.625(5)]; and sexually transmitted diseases [Ky. Rev. Stat. §§ 211.180, 214.410, and 214.420].

State	Health Care Privacy Statute/Provisions	Specific Disclosure Rules
LOUISIANA	No general prohibition on disclosure of confidential medical information. Privacy is addressed in statutes covering specific entities or medical conditions. A health care provider–patient privilege exists pertaining to physicians, psychotherapists, pharmacists, hospitals, rape crisis counselors, and others [La. Code of Evidence Art. 510(a), La. Rev. Stat. Ann. § 13:3734 A].	• HMOs may not disclose any information about the diagnosis or treatment of an enrollee or applicant, with exceptions for disclosure of information necessary to carry out the HMO law, for court orders, and to defend against a claim or litigation by the enrollee or applicant [La. Rev. Stat. Ann. § 22:2020]. • Private utilization review agents may not disclose or publish any confidential medical information or individual medical records obtained during UR activities, except to the party requesting UR [La. Rev. Stat. Ann. § 40:2731]. • Specific disclosure rules apply to reports of communicable diseases [La. Rev. Stat. Ann. § 40:3.1]; genetic information [La. .Rev. Stat. Ann. §§ 22:213.7D, 40:1299.6]; reports of cancer [La. Rev. Stat. Ann. §§ 40:1299:85, 40:1299:87]; and HIV test results [La. Rev. Stat. Ann. § 40:1300.14].

continues

State	Health Care Privacy Statute/Provisions	Specific Disclosure Rules
MAINE	An individual's health care information is confidential and may not be disclosed by a health care practitioner or facility without the person's consent, except as provided by law [Me. Rev. Stat. tit. 22, § 1711-C]. Provider–patient privileges include those of patients of physicians and psychotherapists [Me. R. Rev. R. 503 (privilege expanded to remove rebuttal exceptions in criminal proceedings, April 11, 2002)], and social workers and marriage-family therapists [Me. Rev. Stat. tit. 32, §§ 7005 and 13862].	• Health care practitioners or facilities may disclose information without consent: to other providers and facilities within and outside the original office or practice (except information about mental health services); in quality assurance, utilization or peer reviews; to family members, in certain situations; to third parties when there is a threat of imminent harm to an individual; pursuant to court order or subpoena; for scientific research purposes; and to regulators or those involved in accreditation or certification of a practitioner or facility [Me. Rev. Stat. tit. 22, § 1711-C]. • HMOs may disclose an enrollee's or applicant's health information without consent in order to comply with the HMO laws, pursuant to statute or court order, to assist health care review committees, and in response to a claim or litigation between an enrollee/applicant and the HMO [Me. Rev. Stat. Ann. tit. 24-A, § 4224]. • Special disclosure rules apply to alcoholism and drug abuse treatment records [Me. Rev. Stat. tit. 24-A § 2842]; child abuse incidents [Me. Rev. Stat. tit. 22 § 4015]; communicable disease reporting [Me. Rev. Stat. tit. 22, §§ 815, 821 through 824]; cancer reporting [Me. Rev. Stat. tit. 22, § 1404]; DNA records [Me. Rev. Stat. tit. 25, § 1577]; and HIV test results [Me. Rev. Stat. tit. 5, §§ 19203 and 19203-D].

State	Health Care Privacy Statute/Provisions	Specific Disclosure Rules
MARYLAND	Medical records are confidential and may be disclosed by health care providers only as provided by law [Md. Code Ann. Health-Gen §§ 4-302 and 4-303]. A health care provider-patient privilege is extended only to psychiatrists or psychologists [Md. Court and Judicial Proceedings Code Ann. § 9-109].	• Providers may disclose information without consent; to the provider's employees or agents to provide or seek payment for health care; to the provider's insurer and attorneys, in certain instances; in a health emergency; for educational or research purposes, evaluation of health care delivery systems, or for accreditation purposes; to other providers for purposes of treating the patient; and to organ and tissue procurement entities [Md. Code Ann. Health-Gen § 4-305]. Disclosure of the medical record is mandatory in some circumstances [Md. Code Ann. Health-Gen § 4-306]. • Insurers may disclose an insured's medical records to a medical review committee, accreditation board, or commission; pursuant to court order or subpoena; to a health service plan to coordinate benefits; to investigate possible insurance fraud; to evaluate an insurance application; to adjust a claim; and to evaluate a claim or suit for personal injury [Md. Code Ann. Insurance § 4-403]. • Nonprofit health service plans or Blue Cross/Blue Shield plans may disclose medical information under similar, but not identical, circumstances as above [Md. Code Ann. Insurance § 14-138]. • Specific disclosure rules apply to HIV/AIDS [Md. Code Ann. Health-Gen §§ 18-338.1 and 18-338.2]; mental health records [Md. Code Ann. Health-Gen § 4-304, 4-307]; and reportable diseases [Md. Code Ann. Health-Gen § 18-205].

continues

State	Health Care Privacy Statute/Provisions	Specific Disclosure Rules
MASSACHUSETTS	There is a statutory right of privacy that generally encompasses medical records and information [Mass Gen. Laws ch. 214, § 1B], as well as other statutes governing specific entities and medical conditions. Hospital and other facilities' records are confidential to the extent provided by law, with certain exceptions [Mass. Gen. Laws ch. 111, § 70E]. There is a health provider–patient privilege extended to psychiatrists, psychologists, and psychiatric nurse clinicians, as well as social workers [Mass. Gen. Laws ch. 233, § 20B; Mass Gen. Laws ch. 112, § 135B].	• Physicians, health care facilities, nursing homes, and other providers may disclose patient information without consent to establish eligibility for government benefits, for mandatory health department reports, or as required by any law [Mass Gen. Laws ch. 112, § 12G]. • Insurance entities may disclose information without a person's consent in order to verify insurance benefits; to conduct business when disclosure is necessary; to law enforcement agencies in fraud investigations; and pursuant to search warrant or subpoena [Mass. Gen. Laws ch. 175I, § 4]. • Specific disclosure rules apply to HIV/AIDS testing [Mass. Gen. Laws ch. 111, § 70F]; mental health information [Mass. Gen. Laws ch. 112, § 129A; ch. 123, § 36; and ch. 176G, § 4B]; and infectious disease reports [Mass. Gen. Laws ch. 111D, § 6].

State	Health Care Privacy Statute/Provisions	Specific Disclosure Rules
MICHIGAN	No general prohibition on disclosure of confidential medical information. Specific prohibitions against disclosure apply to certain entities and medical conditions. Information regarding mental health treatment is confidential, with certain exceptions [Mich. Comp. Laws § 330.1748]. Health care provider–patient privileges include psychiatrist or psychologist–patient [Mich. Comp. Laws §§ 330.1700 and 330.1750], physician-patient [Mich. Comp. Laws § 600.2157], licensed professional counselor-client [Mich. Comp. Laws § 333.18117], psychologist-client [Mich. Comp. Laws § 330.1750], and dentist-patient [Mich. Comp. Laws § 333.16648].	• Nonprofit health care corporations may not disclose medical records without patient consent, except for claims adjudication or verifications, or as required by law [Mich. Comp. Laws § 550.1406]. • Third-party claims administrators may not disclose records that contain identifying information about a plan member's diagnosis or treatment without consent, except for claims adjudication or verification, for plan administration, for an ERISA audit, for excess loss insurance purchase or claims, to the insurance commissioner, or as otherwise required by law [Mich. Comp. Laws § 550.934]. • Specific disclosure rules apply to HIV/AIDS [Mich. Comp. Laws § 333.5131]; cancer [Mich. Comp. Laws § 333.2619]; pharmacies [Mich. Comp. Laws § 333.17752]; substance abuse treatment [Mich. Comp. Laws §§ 333.6111 through 333.6113]; and medical research projects [Mich. Comp. Laws § 333.2631].

continues

State	Health Care Privacy Statute/Provisions	Specific Disclosure Rules
MINNESOTA	Health care providers may not release a patient's health records to anyone without patient consent unless specifically authorized by law, with certain exceptions [Minn. Stat. § 144.335 subd. 3a]. Medical records maintained by hospitals and other medical facilities are confidential, with certain exceptions [Minn. Stat. § 144.651 subd. 16]. A health care provider–patient privilege is extended to physicians, nurses, dentists, chiropractors, psychologists, and sexual assault counselors and their patients and clients [Minn. Stat. § 595.02 subd. 1].	• Providers may release health records without consent in a medical emergency, to other providers within related entities for treatment of the patient, and to researchers for medical or scientific research [Minn. Stat. § 144.335 subd. 3a]. • Hospitals and other health facilities may disclose without consent where required by third-party payment contracts, in complaint inspections and health department inspections, and as otherwise provided by law [Minn. Stat. § 144.651 subd. 16]. • HMOs may disclose privileged information in some circumstances: to detect or prevent fraud; to verify insurance coverage, inform a person of a health problem, or conduct an operations audit; to insurance regulators; to law enforcement officials in the event of fraud or other illegal activities; and pursuant to a search warrant or subpoena [Minn. Stat. § 72A.502 subd. 2 through 11]. • Specific disclosure rules apply to genetic information [Minn. Stat. § 72A.139], cancer reporting [Minn. Stat. § 144.671], and records maintained by the government [Minn. Stat. §§ 13.02 subd. 12, 13.04, 13.3805 subd. 1].

State	Health Care Privacy Statute/Provisions	Specific Disclosure Rules
MISSISSIPPI	No general prohibition on disclosure of confidential medical information. Specific prohibitions against disclosure apply to certain entities and medical conditions. Hospital records are privileged communications [Miss. Code Ann. § 41-9-67]. Health care provider-patient privileges extend to physicians, osteopaths, hospital, nurses, pharmacists, podiatrists, optometrists, and chiropractors and their patients [Miss. Code Ann. § 13-1-21], and to psychotherapists and psychologists [Miss. Code Ann. § 73-31-29, Miss. R.E. 503].	• HMOs and other benefit plans may disclose medical information without the person's consent to the extent necessary to follow the law governing such plans; pursuant to statute or court order; and in the event of claim or litigation between the person and the HMO [Miss. Code Ann. § 83-41-355]. • Mental health records are confidential and may be released without patient consent only upon court order; when necessary for the patient's continuing treatment; when necessary to determine eligibility for benefits, compliance with statutory reporting requirements, or other lawful purpose; and when the patient has threatened imminent violence to an identifiable victim [Miss. Code Ann. § 41-21-97]. • Specific disclosure rules apply to alcoholism treatment [Miss. Code Ann. § 41-30-33]; birth defects registry [Miss. Code Ann. § 41-21-205]; and cancer registry [Miss. Code Ann. § 41-91-5].

continues

State	Health Care Privacy Statute/Provisions	Specific Disclosure Rules
MISSOURI	No general prohibition on disclosure of confidential medical information. A number of health care provider–patient privileges are extended [Mo. Rev. Stat. §§ 337.055 (psychologist); 337.540 (professional counselor); 337.636 (social worker); 337.736 (marital and family counselor); and 491.060 (physician, chiropractor, psychologist, and dentist)].	• HMOs may disclose an enrollee's or applicant's medical information without consent in order to follow the law governing HMOs; in response to a claim or litigation between the person and the HMO; and pursuant to statute or court order [Mo. Rev. Stat. § 354.515]. • Specific disclosure rules apply to mental health facilities and programs [Mo. Rev. Stat. § 630.140]; pharmacies [Mo. Rev. Stat. § 338.100]; epidemiological study data [Mo. Rev. Stat. § 192.067]; cancer reporting [Mo. Rev. Stat. §§ 192.650 and 192.655]; abuse and neglect of adults [Mo. Rev. Stat. § 660.263] and children [Mo. Rev. Stat. §§ 210.115 (reporting requirement expanded to include ministers) and 210.150]; HIV/AIDS [Mo. Rev. Stat. §§ 191.653 and 191.656 (disclosure exception expanded to include prosecutors and victims of sexual offenses)]; and genetic and metabolic information [Mo. Rev. Stat. §§ 191.323, 375.1309].

State	Health Care Privacy Statute/Provisions	Specific Disclosure Rules
MONTANA	A provider may not disclose health care information about a patient to any other person without the patient's written authorization [Mont. Code Ann. § 50-16-525]. A number of provider-patient privileges are extended [Mont. Code Ann., §§ 26-1-805 (physician–patient), 26-1-806 (speech/language pathologist–client), and 26-1-807 (psychologist-client)].	• A provider may disclose patient health information without consent to a person providing health care to the patient; for purposes of health care education, planning, quality assurance, peer review, or administrative services to the provider; to family members or close friends of the patient; to successor health care providers; for use in approved research projects; for an audit; to officials of a custodial institution in which the patient is detained; where there is a risk of immediate danger to an individual's health or safety; as required by law; or pursuant to subpoena or court order [Mont. Code Ann. §§ 60-16-529 and 50-16-530]. • HMOs may not disclose any information about an enrollee's or applicant's treatment or health without express consent, with certain exceptions [Mont. Code Ann. § 33-31-113]. • Insurance entities may disclose a person's medical information only under certain circumstances: to verify insurance benefits; when necessary to conduct business; to law enforcement agencies in fraud situations; pursuant to search warrant or subpoena; and for marketing purposes, with certain restrictions [Mont. Code Ann. § 33-19-306]. • Specific disclosure rules apply to HIV testing [Mont. Code Ann. § 50-16-1009]; infant mortality [Mont. Code Ann. § 50-16-102]; artificial insemination [Mont. Code Ann. § 40-6-106]; mental health [Mont. Code Ann. §§ 63-21-141, 53-21-166]; and sexually transmitted diseases [Mont. Code Ann. § 50-18-109].

continues

State	Health Care Privacy Statute/Provisions	Specific Disclosure Rules
NEBRASKA	No general prohibition on disclosure of confidential medical information. Privacy protections are contained in statutes governing specific medical conditions and entities [Neb. Rev. Stat. §§ 44-7210 (health carrier); 44-32, 172 (HMO); 44-4110.01 (preferred provider); and 44-4725 (prepaid limited health service)]. Physician–patient and professional counselor-client privileges exist [Neb. Rules of Evidence, Rule 504].	• Health carriers and plans may only disclose enrollee/applicant health information without consent under limited circumstances: as necessary to carry out the laws governing the entity; pursuant to court order; and in order to defend against a claim or litigation by the covered person [Neb. Rev. Stat. §§ 44-7210, 44-32, 172, 44-4110.01, and 44-4725]. • Mental health professionals may disclose client or patient information without consent only pursuant to the rules of the Board of Examiners; when the person has brought charges against the provider; or when a patient has made a serious threat of violence against him or herself or an identifiable victim [Neb. Rev. Stat. §§ 71-1,335 and 71-1,336]. • Specific disclosure rules apply to pharmacists [Neb. Rev. Stat. § 71-1,157.36]; state registries for birth defects, brain injuries, and cancer [Neb. Rev. Stat. §§ 71-646, 81-669, 81-653 through 81-659, 81-642 through 81-647]; communicable diseases [Neb. Rev. Stat. §§ 71-502 through 71-503.01, 71-532, 71-507 through 71-511]; and morbidity/mortality studies [Neb. Rev. Stat. § 71-3402].

State	Health Care Privacy Statute/Provisions	Specific Disclosure Rules
NEVADA	No general prohibition on disclosure of confidential medical information. Restrictions on disclosure are found in statutes governing specific entities or conditions. A number of health care provider–patient privileges exist [Nev. Rev. Stat. §§ 49.225 and 49.215 (physician, dentist, osteopath, and psychiatric social worker); 49.209 (psychol-ogist); 49.247 (marriage and family therapy); and 49.252 (social worker)].	• Mental health records of institutionalized patients are confidential, with certain exceptions [Nev. Rev. Stat. §§ 433A.360, 433.482(8)]. • Group insurers are prohibited from disclosing to the policyholder the fact that an insured is taking a prescribed drug or the identity of that drug [Nev. Rev. Stat. § 689B.280]. • Prepaid limited health service organizations may only disclose medical information of an enrollee without consent pursuant to statute or court order; to carry out the law governing such entities; or for a claim of legal action [Nev. Rev. Stat. § 695F.410]. • Specific disclosure rules apply to pharmacists [Nev. Rev. Stat. § 639.238]; reporting of communicable diseases [Nev. Rev. Stat. §§ 441A.150, 441A.220 and 441A.230]; genetic information [Nev. Rev. Stat. §§ 396.521 and 396.523, 629.161]; and epilepsy [Nev. Rev. Stat. § 439.270].

continues

State	Health Care Privacy Statute/Provisions	Specific Disclosure Rules
NEW HAMPSHIRE	No general prohibition on disclosure of confidential medical information. Statutes governing specific entities or medical conditions contain restrictions on disclosure. Information in a patient's hospital clinical record is confidential [N.H. Rev. Stat. § 151:21 X]. Numerous health care privileges exist [N.H. Rev. Stat. §§ 329.26 (physician); 316-A:27 (chiropractor); 326-B:30 (nurse); 328-F:28 (allied health professional); and 330-A:32 (mental health practitioner)].	• Health carriers offering managed care plans may not disclose health information of a covered person without consent except: to the extent necessary to carry out the law governing health carriers; pursuant to statute or court order; or in the event of claim or litigation between the person and the carrier [N.H. Rev. Stat. § 420-J:10]. • Specific disclosure rules apply to marketing of provider services [N.H. Rev. Stat. § 332-I:1]; pharmacists [N.H. Rev. Stat. § 318.29]; medical and scientific research [N.H. Rev. Stat. § 126-A:11]; HIV [N.H. Rev. Stat. §§ 141-F:7 and 141-F:8]; cancer reporting [N.H. Rev. Stat. §§ 141-B:7 and 141-B:9]; communicable diseases [N.H. Rev. Stat. §§ 141-C:7 and 141-C:8]; and genetic testing [N.H. Rev. Stat. § 141-H:2].

State	Health Care Privacy Statute/Provisions	Specific Disclosure Rules
NEW JERSEY	A hospital patient has a right to confidentiality of all records pertaining to his or her treatment except as otherwise provided by law or third-party payment contract [N.J. Stat. 26:2H-12.8]. Privacy protections are founded in statutes governing specific entities and medical conditions. A number of health care provider–patient privileges exist [N.J. Stat. §§ 2A:84A-22.1 and 2A:84A-22.2 (physician); 45-14B-28 (psychologist); and 45:8B-29 (marriage/family therapist)]. HMOs, dental plans, and prepaid prescription services may claim any privilege the original provider of the information is entitled to claim. [N.J. Stat. §§ 17:48D-21, 17:48F-28 and 26:2J-27].	• HMOs may disclose enrollee/applicant medical information without consent only to the extent necessary to carry out the law governing HMOs; pursuant to statute or court order; or in the event of claim or litigation between the person and the HMO [N.J. Stat. § 26-2J-27]. • An insurance entity may not disclose medical information about a person without consent, with certain exceptions: verifying insurance coverage benefits to a medical professional; to agents for purpose of conducting the entity's business when disclosure is necessary; to law enforcement agencies in fraud investigations; and pursuant to court order [N.J. Stat. § 17-23A-1 through 17-23A-18]. • Utilization review committees may disclose information they receive only to: a patient's attending physician; the CAO of the facility it serves; the facility's enforcement unit; government agencies in the performance of their duties; and the patient's insurer or plan, if authorized by the terms of coverage [N.J. Stat. § 2A:84A-22.8]. • Specific disclosure rules apply to state cancer and birth defects registries [N.J. Stat. §§ 26:8-40:23, 26:2-107]; genetic information [N.J. Stat. § 10:5-47]; HIV/AIDS [N.J. Stat. §§ 26:5C-7 and 26:5C-8]; venereal disease [N.J. Stat. § 26:4-41]; and institutionalized mentally ill persons [N.J. Stat. § 30:4-24.3].

State	Health Care Privacy Statute/Provisions	Specific Disclosure Rules
NEW MEXICO	No general prohibition on disclosure of confidential medical information. Privacy protections are found in statutes governing specific entities and medical conditions. Numerous provider–patient privileges exist [N.M.R. of Evid. 11-504 (physician and psychotherapist), R. 11-509 (social worker); N.M. Stat. Ann. §§ 31-25-3 (victim counselor), and 61-9-18 (psychologist)].	• HMOs may not disclose enrollee/applicant health information without consent, with certain exceptions: to the extent necessary to comply with the HMO law; pursuant to court order; or in order to defend against claims or litigation by the enrollee/applicant [N.M. Stat. Ann. § 49A-46-27]. • All hospital records and health information that relates to and identifies specific persons as patients is confidential and not a matter of public record even if the information is in the custody or contained in records of a governmental agency; a custodian of confidential information may furnish it upon request to a governmental agency, a state educational institution, an association of licensed physicians, a licensed health facility, or staff committee [N.M. Stat. Ann. § 14-6-1]. • Specific disclosure rules apply to mental illness and developmental disabilities [N.M. Stat. Ann. § 43-1-19]; sexually transmitted diseases and HIV [N.M. Stat. Ann. §§ 24-1-9.4, 24-2B-6]; and genetic information [N.M. Stat. Ann. § 24-21-3].

State	Health Care Privacy Statute/Provisions	Specific Disclosure Rules
NEW YORK	No general prohibition on disclosure of confidential medical information. Nursing homes and facilities providing health services must adopt and publish a statement of a patient's right to have confidentiality in treatment of personal and medical records [N.Y. Pub. Health Law § 2803-c 3]. A number of health care provider-patient privileges exist [N.Y. C.P.L.R. 4504 (physicians, nurses, dentists, podiatrists, chiropractors, medical corporations, professional service corporations, and university faculty practices); 4507 (psychologists); 4508 (social workers); and 4510 (rape crisis counselor)].	• Upon request of an insured or prospective insured, insurers must provide their procedures for protecting the confidentiality of medical records [N.Y. Ins. Law § 3217-a(b)(5)]. • When disclosing patient information to a person other than the patient, a health care provider must make a notation of the purpose of the disclosure, which must be as authorized by law, but a notation is not required for disclosure to practitioners or employees or agents of the facility or to government agencies inspecting the facility or investigating professional conduct [N.Y. Pub. Health Law § 18(6)]. These provisions also apply to HMOs [N.Y. Pub. Health Law § 18(1)(c), 4410]. • Utilization review agents must have written procedures assuring confidentiality of patient-specific information obtained during UR, and may disclose the information only as authorized by law [N.Y. Ins. Law § 4905(a)]. • Specific disclosure rules apply to child abuse reports by HMOs [N.Y. Pub. Health Law § 4410.3]; records of mental health treatment [N.Y. Mental Hyg. Law § 33.13]; HIV/AIDS test results [N.Y. Pub. Health Law §§ 2781 and 2782]; communicable diseases including HIV [N.Y. Pub. Health Law §§ 2102, 2134-2135]; Alzheimer's disease [N.Y. Pub. Health Law §§ 2003]; cancer cases [N.Y. Pub. Health Law § 2402]; and birth defects and genetic allied diseases [N.Y. Pub. Health Law § 2733].

continues

State	Health Care Privacy Statute/Provisions	Specific Disclosure Rules
NORTH CAROLINA	No general prohibition on disclosure of confidential medical information, but disclosure of confidential medical information by insurance entities, including HMOs, and mental health facilities, is restricted by specific statutes. Several health care provider-patient privileges exist [N.C. Gen. Stat. §§ 8-53 (physician–patient), 8-53.3 (psychologist–client), 8-53.5 (marital/family therapist–client), 8-53.7 (social worker–client), and 8-53.8 (professional counselor–client)].	• Medical records compiled and maintained by health care facilities in connection with individual patients are not public records and are not subject to inspection [N.C. Gen. Stat. § 131E-97]. • HMOs may not disclose enrollee/applicant health information without consent, except to the extent necessary to comply with the HMO law; pursuant to statute or court order; or in a claim or litigation between the person and the HMO [N.C. Gen. Stat. § 58-67-180]. • Insurance entities, including HMOs and medical service corporations, may not disclose a person's medical information without authorization, with limited exceptions: verifying insurance benefits; to conduct business when the disclosure is necessary; to law enforcement agencies in preventing or prosecuting fraud; and pursuant to a search warrant or subpoena [N.C. Gen. Stat. §§ 58-39-75(2) through (20)]. • Specific disclosure rules apply to pharmacies [N.C. Gen. Stat. § 90-85.36]; mental health, developmental disabilities and substance abuse treatment facilities [N.C. Gen. Stat. §§ 122C-3, 122C-51 through 122C-56, 122C-25]; and communicable diseases including HIV [N.C. Gen. Stat. §§ 130A-135 through 130A-140, 130A-143].

State	Health Care Privacy Statute/Provisions	Specific Disclosure Rules
NORTH DAKOTA	No general prohibition on disclosure of confidential medical information. Privacy protections are found in statutes governing various entities and medical conditions. Several health care provider–patient privileges exist [N.D. Rules of Evidence, Rule 501, 503 (physician and psychotherapist–patient); N.D. Cent. Code §§ 31-01-06.3 (addiction counselor–client), and 43-47-09 (licensed professional counselor–client)].	• Hospitals and other facilities providing maternity care may disclose the contents of their records in a judicial proceeding, to health or social agencies specifically interested in the patients, and to persons with a direct interest in the patient or infant's well-being [N.D. Cent. Code § 23-16-09]. • Insurers, HMOs, and other health plan entities must maintain procedures to ensure that all identifiable information regarding covered persons remains confidential, and may not disclose enrollee/applicant health information without consent, except: as necessary to follow the law governing the entity; pursuant to court order; or to defend against claims or litigation by the person [N.D. Cent. Code §§ 26.1-36-03.1, 26.1-36-12.4]. • Specific disclosure rules apply to abortion records [N.D. Cent. Code § 14-02.1-07]; HIV/AIDS [N.D. Cent. Code §§ 23-07.5-05, 23-07-02.1 and 23-07-02.2]; congenital deformity reports [N.D. Cent. Code § 50-10-07]; research studies on morbidity and mortality [N.D. Cent. Code § 23-01-15]; and sexually transmitted disease [N.D. Cent. Code §§ 23-07-03, 23-07-20.1].

continues

State	Health Care Privacy Statute/Provisions	Specific Disclosure Rules
OHIO	No general prohibition on disclosure of confidential medical information. Privacy protections are found in statutes governing specific medical conditions or entities. Several health care provider–patient privileges exist [Oh. Rev. Code § 2317.02 (physicians, dentists, chiropractors, professional counselors, social workers) and Oh. Rev. Code § 4732.19 (psychologists)].	• Insurance entities may not disclose a person's medical information without authorization except: to verify coverage benefits to a medical professional; to agents in conducting business when disclosure is necessary; to law enforcement agencies in order to prevent or prosecute fraud; pursuant to a search warrant or subpoena; and for marketing purposes, with certain restrictions [Oh. Rev. Code § 3904.13]. • Quality assurance and utilization review committees may use confidential records and information made available to them only in the exercise of committee functions [Oh. Rev. Code § 2305.24]. • Physicians, physician assistants, and psychologists may not disclose confidential communications, and may be subject to disciplinary action for doing so [Oh. Rev. Code §§ 4730.25, 4731.22, 4732.17 and 4732.19]. • Specific disclosure rules apply to HIV/AIDS [Oh. Rev. Code § 3701.243]; long-term care resident records [Oh. Rev. Code § 173.20]; mental illness and mental retardation [Oh. Rev. Code § 5122.31]; and cancer registry [Oh. Rev. Code § 3701.262].

State	Health Care Privacy Statute/Provisions	Specific Disclosure Rules
OKLAHOMA	No general prohibition on disclosure of confidential medical information. Privacy protections are found in statutes governing certain medical conditions or entities. Several provider–patient privileges exist [Okla. Stat. tit. 12, § 2503 (physician and psychotherapist–patient); Okla. Stat. tit. 59, §§ 1272.1 (social worker–client), 1910 (licensed professional counselor–client), and 1925.11 (family therapist–patient)].	• Medical records and communications between a physician or psychotherapist and a mental health client are confidential and may not be disclosed without the patient's consent except by court order, or to other persons or agencies actively engaged in the patient's treatment or in related administrative work [Okla. Stat. tit. 43A, § 1-109 (expanded to include drug or alcohol abuse treatment information, mandatory reporting of child abuse and other such crimes)]. • A psychologist may not disclose the fact that a patient is undergoing treatment, information acquired during treatment, or records of treatment without consent except in limited circumstances, such as when the patient has threatened to kill an identified person [Okla. Stat. tit. 59, § 1376]. • Specific disclosure rules apply to venereal diseases [Okla. Stat. tit. 63, § 1-502.2] and to the state tumor registry [Okla. Stat. tit. 63, § 1-551.1].

continues

State	Health Care Privacy Statute/Provisions	Specific Disclosure Rules
OREGON	Personal medical information is exempt from public disclosure unless the public interest, by clear and convincing evidence, requires disclosure in a particular instance [Or. Rev. Stat. § 192.502]. Several provider–patient privileges exist [Or. Rev. Stat. §§ 40.230 (psycho-therapists), 40.235 (physicians), 40.240 (nurses), 40.250 (clinical social workers), and 40.262 (counselors)].	• Insurers may not disclose any personal or privileged information about a person without written authorization, with certain exceptions: to verify insurance benefits; to conduct business when disclosure is necessary; to law enforcement agencies in preventing or prosecuting fraud; or pursuant to court order [Or. Rev. Stat. §§ 746.655(b) through (q)]. • Specific disclosure rules apply to alcohol and drug abuse treatment [Or. Rev. Stat. § 430.399]; cancer registry [Or. Rev. Stat. § 432.520]; genetic testing [Or. Rev. Stat. § 192.539]; HIV status [Or. Rev. Stat. § 433.045]; mental health records [Or. Rev. Stat. § 179.505]; reportable diseases [Or. Rev. Stat. §§ 433.004 and 433.008]; and morbidity and mortality studies [Or. Rev. Stat. § 432.060].

State	Health Care Privacy Statute/Provisions	Specific Disclosure Rules
PENNSYLVANIA	No general prohibition on disclosure of confidential medical information. Privacy protections are found in statutes governing specific medical conditions or entities. A number of mental health care provider–patient privileges exist [42 Pa. Cons. Stat. §§ 5944 (psychiatrist/psychologist) and 5945 (school nurses and school psychologists)]. There is also a narrowly drawn physician–patient privilege [42 Pa. Cons. Stat. § 5929].	• Managed care plans and utilization review entities must maintain procedures to ensure that all identifiable information regarding enrollee treatment and health remains confidential. Disclosure is permitted to determine coverage, review complaints, conduct utilization review, or facilitate payment of a claim [40 Pa. Cons. Stat. 2102, 2131]. • Specific disclosure rules apply to alcohol and drug abuse treatment [71 Pa. Cons. Stat. § 1690.108]; cancer reporting [35 Pa. Cons. Stat. § 5636]; HIV/AIDS [35 Pa. Cons. Stat. § 7607]; communicable diseases [35 Pa. Cons. Stat. §§ 521.4, 521.15]; and mental health [50 Pa. Cons. Stat. §§ 7103 and 7111].

continues

State	Health Care Privacy Statute/Provisions	Specific Disclosure Rules
RHODE ISLAND	The Confidentiality of Health Care Communications and Information Act provides a general, comprehensive prohibition against disclosure of confidential health care information [R.I. Gen. Laws §§ 5-37.3-3 and 5-37.3-4]. It includes information obtained from any health care service provider, including physicians, hospitals, dentists, optometrists, social workers, psychologists, and others. The physician–patient privilege is governed by the provisions of the Act.	• Confidential medical information may be released without patient consent under numerous circumstances, including: peer review boards; providers for coordinating health care services for the patient and for education and training within the facility; scientific research, with restrictions; news media (limited to the fact of a patient's hospital admission and general description of his or her condition); the provider's lawyer if the patient sues the provider for medical liability; and others [R.I. Gen. Laws § 5-37.3-4(b)]. • Managed care entities and contractors are prohibited from providing any identifying information to any medical information data base unless essential to compile statistical data regarding enrollees [R.I. Gen. Laws § 5-37.3-4(a)]. • Specific disclosure rules apply to genetic information [R.I. Gen. Laws § 28-6.7-1 (requirement of genetic testing or disclosure of genetic information generally prohibited; prohibitions greatly expanded, June 8, 2002)]; HIV/AIDS [R.I. Gen. Laws § 23-6-17]; state cancer registry [R.I. Gen. Laws § 23-12-4]; and mental health [R.I. Gen. Laws §§ 40.1-5-26 and 40.1-5-27].

State	Health Care Privacy Statute/Provisions	Specific Disclosure Rules
SOUTH CAROLINA	No general prohibition on disclosure of confidential medical information. Privacy protections are found in laws governing specific medical conditions and entities. The physician–patient privilege is not recognized, but there is a mental health professional–client privilege [S.C. Code § 44-22-90].	• Physicians, hospitals, and other health facilities must provide the health department, upon request, access to their medical records, tumor registries, and other special disease record systems as necessary for its investigations [S.C. Code Ann- § 44-1-110]. • In responding to a request for medical information from an insurer, a physician may rely on the carrier's representation that the patient has authorized release of the information [S.C. Code § 44-115-50]. • A physician may sell medical records to another licensed physician or osteopath, but must first publish notice of his or her intention and of the patient's right to retrieve his or her records before a sale [S.C. Code § 44-115-130]. • Specific disclosure rules apply to genetic information [S.C. Code § 38-93-30]; sexually transmitted diseases [S.C. Code §§ 44-29-70, 44-29-135 and 44-29-136]; mental health [S.C. Code § 44-22-90]; and cancer reports [S.C. Code § 44-35-40].

continues

State	Health Care Privacy Statute/Provisions	Specific Disclosure Rules
SOUTH DAKOTA	No general prohibition on disclosure of confidential medical information. Prohibitions are addressed in laws governing specific entities and medical conditions, There are several provider–patient privileges [S.D. Codified Laws §§ 19-13-6 and 19-13-7 (physician/psychoanalysts); § 34-20A-90 (alcohol and drug treatment facilities); § 36-26-30 (social workers); and § 36-32-27 (professional counselors)].	• HMOs may disclose enrollee/applicant health information without consent only to the extent necessary to follow the HMO law; pursuant to statute or court order; or in a claim or litigation between the person and the HMO [S.D. Codified Laws § 58-41-73]. • Specific disclosure rules apply to communicable diseases [S.D. Codified Laws § 34-22-12]; child abuse reports [S.D. Codified Laws § 26-8A-13]; alcohol and drug abuse [S.D. Codified Laws § 34-20A-90]; venereal disease [S.D. Codified Laws § 34-23-2]; mental health information [S.D. Codified Laws § 27A-12-26]; and cancer reports [S.D. Codified Laws §§ 1-43-11, 1-43-16 and 34-14-1].

State	Health Care Privacy Statute/Provisions	Specific Disclosure Rules
TENNESSEE	No general prohibition on disclosure of confidential medical Information. Privacy is addressed in statutes governing specific entities and medical conditions. There is no physician–patient privilege, but a number of mental health care provider–patient privileges exist [Tenn. Code Ann. §§ 24-1-207 (psychiatrist–patient); 63-11-213 (psychologist/mental health professional–patient); 63-22-114 (marital/family therapist–client); and 63-23-107 (social worker–client)].	• Health care providers (including physicians, chiropractors, dentists, nurses, pharmacists, optometrists, professional counselors, and other licensed professionals) may not disclose a patient's name and address or other identifying information except in specified circumstances: statutorily required reports to health or government authorities; to third-party payors for utilization review, case management, peer reviews, or other administrative functions; and pursuant to subpoena [Tenn. Code Ann. § 63-2-101(b)]. • Hospitals and clinics may not disclose patient information except: mandatory reports to health authorities; for utilization reviews, case management or other administrative functions; pursuant to subpoena; or to providers treating the patient [Tenn, Code Ann. § 68-11-1502]. • Specific disclosure rules apply to abortions [Tenn. Code Ann. § 39-15-203]; genetic information [Tenn. Code Ann. §§ 56-7-2702 and 56-7-2704]; sexually transmitted diseases and HIV [Tenn. Code Ann. §§ 68-10-113 and 68-10-115]; mental health records [Tenn. Code Ann. § 33-3-104(10)]; and cancer registry [Tenn. Code Ann. §§ 688-1-1003 and 67-1-1006].

continues

State	Health Care Privacy Statute/Provisions	Specific Disclosure Rules
TEXAS	No general prohibition on disclosure of confidential medical information. Privacy is addressed in laws governing specific entities and medical conditions. A physician's treatment records and communications with a patient are confidential and may not be disclosed except as allowed by statute without the patient's consent [Tex. Occ. Code § 159.001 *et seq.*]. Numerous health care provider–patient privileges exist [Tex. R. Evid. 509 (physicians); Tex. Health & Safety Code §§ 611.002 and 611.003 (mental health professionals)].	• HMOs may disclose enrollee/applicant health information without consent only as necessary to follow the law governing HMOs; pursuant to statute or court order; or in a claim or litigation between the person and the HMO [Tex. Ins. Code art. 20A.25]. (Note: Repealed by Acts 2001, Ch. 1419, § 31(b)(13), effective June 1, 2003). • Hospitals may disclose a patient's health information without written consent only to a provider attending the patient; to an organ or tissue organization; and to specified others [Tex. Health and Safety Code §§ 241.152 and 241.153]. • Specific disclosure laws apply to communicable diseases [Tex. Health and Safety Code §§ 81.041, 81.046, and 81.203]; state cancer registry [Tex. Health and Safety Code § 82.009]; mental health records; [Tex. Health and Safety Code §§ 611.002 and 611.004]; sexual assault advocacy services [Tex. Health and Safety Code §§ 44.071 and 44.072]; HIV test results [Tex. Health and Safety Code § 81.103]; and occupational conditions [Tex. Health and Safety Code §§ 84.001, 84.006].

State	Health Care Privacy Statute/Provisions	Specific Disclosure Rules
UTAH	No general prohibition on disclosure of confidential medical information. Records maintained by a governmental entity that contain individuals' medical information are private records and not open to public inspection, but must be disclosed under certain enumerated circumstances [Utah Code Ann. §§ 63-2-201 and 63-2-202]. Several provider–patient privileges exist. [Utah Code Ann. §§ 78-24-8(4) (physicians) and 78-24-8(6) (sexual assault counselors); and Utah Rules of Evidence, Rule 506 (mental health therapists)].	• Psychologists, mental health therapists, and substance abuse counselors may disclose confidential communications with a patient without consent under certain limited circumstances: in reporting certain conditions as required by law; as part of an administrative, civil, or criminal proceeding; or under a professional or ethical standard that authorizes or requires disclosure (Utah Code Ann. §§ 58-61-602, 58-60-114, and 58-60-509]. • Specific disclosure rules apply to communicable diseases, including venereal diseases and HIV [Utah Code Ann. §§ 26-6-6, 26-6-3.5, 26-6-16, and 26-6-27]; sexual assault counseling [Utah Code Ann. § 78-3c-4]; and abuse or neglect of vulnerable adults [Utah Code Ann. §§ 62A-3-311 and 62A-3-311.1].

continues

State	Health Care Privacy Statute/Provisions	Specific Disclosure Rules
VERMONT	No general prohibition on disclosure of confidential medical records. Privacy protections found in laws governing specific medical conditions and entities. Hospital patients have a right to privacy of their hospital records and communications [18 Vt. Stat. Ann. § 1852(a)]. Several health care provider–patient privileges exist, extending to a patient and his or her physician, chiropractor, dentist, nurse, psychologist, social worker, mental health counselor, or other mental health professional [12 Ct. Stat. Ann. § 1612; 18 Vt. Stat. Ann. § 7101(13); and Vt. Rules of Evidence, Rule 503].	• Disclosure of hospital records without patient authorization is allowed only to medical personnel directly treating the patient, or to persons monitoring the quality of the treatment or researching its effectiveness [18 Vt. Stat. Ann. § 1852(a)]. • Specific disclosure rules apply to research data [1 Vt. Stat. Ann. § 317(c)(23)]; communicable diseases and HIV reporting [18 Vt. Stat. Ann. § 1001]; cancer and mammography registries [18 Ct. Stat. Ann. §§ 152 to 157]; and mental illness [18 Vt. Stat. Ann. § 7103].

State	Health Care Privacy Statute/Provisions	Specific Disclosure Rules
VIRGINIA	No provider or other person working in a health care setting may disclose a patient's records without his or her consent, except when permitted by statute [Va. Code Ann. § 32.1-127.1:03(A) and (D)(1)]. This includes records maintained by physicians, hospitals, dentists, pharmacists, psychologists, professional counselors, HMOs, nursing homes, state-operated health facilities, and others [Va. Code Ann. §§ 8.01-581.1 and 32.1-127.1:03(B)]. Provider–patient privileges exist for physicians and other "licensed practitioner of the healing arts" [Va. Code Ann. § 8.01-399] and for licensed professional counselors, clinical social workers, and psychologists [Va. Code Ann. § 8.01-400.2].	• A provider may disclose a patient's records without consent under certain enumerated circumstances: pursuant to subpoena; as required by law including contagious disease, public safety, and reporting requirements for suspected abuse; in the normal course of business in a standard health services setting; to third-party payors or agents in connection with payment of bills; and others [Va. Code Ann. § 32.1-127.1:03(D)]. • Insurance entities may not disclose a person's medical information without written consent, with certain exceptions: verifying coverage benefits to a medical professional; conducting actuarial or research studies; for conducting business when disclosure is necessary; to law enforcement agencies to prevent or prosecute fraud; and pursuant to court order, including search warrant or subpoena [Va. Code Ann. § 38.2-613]. • Specific disclosure rules apply to cancer reports [Va. Code Ann. §§ 32.1-70 and 32.1-71]; genetic and metabolic diseases [Va. Code Ann. §§ 32.1-65 and 32.1-69, 38.2-508.4, and 38.2-612]; congenital anomalies [Va. Code Ann. §§ 32.1-69.1 and 32.1-69.2]; and mental health [Va. Code Ann. §§ 37.1-226 to 37.1-229].

continues

State	Health Care Privacy Statute/Provisions	Specific Disclosure Rules
WASHINGTON	The Uniform Health Care Information Act [Wash. Rev. Code Ann. § 70.02.005 *et seq.*] governs disclosure of health care information maintained by health care providers, their employees and agents, and restricts them from disclosing such information about a patient to any other person without written authorization [Wash. Rev. Code Ann. § 70.02.020]. A provider–patient privilege is extended to physicians [Wash. Rev. Code Ann. § 5.60.060], psychologists [Wash. Rev. Code Ann. § 18.83.110], and nurses [Wash. Rev. Code Ann. § 5.62.020], among others.	• Health care providers must disclose patient information without consent in certain circumstances: to health authorities as required by law or if needed to determine compliance with licensure laws or to protect the public health; to law enforcement authorities as required by laws; to coroners and medical examiners for investigations of deaths; and pursuant to compulsory process [Wash. Rev. Code Ann. § 70.02.050(2)]. • Providers may disclose health information without patient consent under a variety of circumstances: to a person providing health care to the patient; to persons using the information for health care education, planning, quality assurance, peer review, administrative or other services to the provider; to a provider who previously treated the patient; to any person in the event of imminent danger to the health or safety of the patient or another person; to a patient's immediate family or close friend, if in accordance with good professional practice; to a successor provider; to an approved research project; for an audit; and others [Wash. Rev. Code Ann. § 70.02.050(1)]. • Specific disclosure rules apply to alcoholism and drug addiction treatment [Wash. Rev. Code Ann. § 70.96A.230]; reports of abuse [Wash. Rev. Code Ann. § 26.44.030]; medical research [Wash. Rev. Code Ann. §§ 42.48.010 through 42.48.040]; HIV and sexually transmitted diseases [Wash. Rev. Code Ann. §§ 70.24.022 and 70.24.105]; cancer registry [Wash. Rev. Code Ann. § 70.54.230]; long-term care residents [Wash. Rev. Code Ann. § 43.190.110]; mental health [Wash. Rev. Code Ann. §§ 71.05.390 to 71.05.427, 71.05.610 through 71.05.690]; and others.

State	Health Care Privacy Statute/Provisions	Specific Disclosure Rules
WEST VIRGINIA	No general prohibition on disclosure of confidential medical information. There is no recognized physician–patient privilege.	• Social workers and professional counselors may not disclose any confidential information acquired from clients without the client's consent, except in limited instances such as when the client is contemplating a crime or harmful act [W. Va. Code §§ 30-30-12, 30-31-13]. • HMOs may not disclose enrollee/applicant health information without express consent, except to the extent necessary to follow the law governing HMOs, pursuant to statute or court order, or in a claim or litigation between the person and the HMO [W. Va. Code § 33-25A-26]. • Specific disclosure rules apply to the state cancer registry (W. Va. Code § 16-5A-2a]; pharmacists [W. Va. Code § 30-5-1b]; HIV test results [W. Va. Code § 16-3C-3]; and mental health information [W.Va. Code § 27-3-1].

continues

State	Health Care Privacy Statute/Provisions	Specific Disclosure Rules
WISCONSIN	All patient health care records are confidential, and may be released only as provided by law or with the patient's consent, with certain exceptions [Wis. Stat. Ann. § 146.82]. There is a broad health care provider–patient privilege, extending to physicians, registered nurses, chiropractors, psychologists, social workers, marriage/family therapists, and professional counselors and their patients/clients [Wis. Stat. Ann. § 905.04].	• Patient health care records must be released without the patient's consent in a number of situations: for management audits, program monitoring and accreditation; to providers or persons acting under their supervision; for billing, collection, or payment of claims; pursuant to court order; for research, with certain limitations; to government agencies that require reporting of certain conditions; to county officials in child abuse/neglect investigations; and to specified others [Wis. Stat. Ann. § 146.82]. • An insurer may disclose a person's medical information without the person's consent to a health care facility or provider for verifying insurance coverage or benefits or for an operations or services audit; if necessary to a group policyholder for reporting claims experience; to pursue a subrogation of claim; and others [Wis. Stat. Ann. § 610.70(5)]. • Specific disclosure rules apply to the state cancer registry [Wis. Stat. Ann. § 255.04]; genetic information [Wis. Stat. Ann. § 631.89]; HIV-related information [Wis. Stat. Ann. § 252.15(5)]; mental health, developmental disability, and drug/alcohol abuse treatment records [Wis. Stat. Ann. § 51.30]; congenital disorders [Wis. Stat. Ann. § 253.13]; and sexually transmitted diseases [Wis. Stat. Ann. § 252.11].

State	Health Care Privacy Statute/Provisions	Specific Disclosure Rules
WYOMING	No general prohibition on disclosure of confidential medical information. A number of health care provider–patient privileges exist [Wyo. Stat. Ann. §§ 1-12-101 (physician-patient); 33-27-123 (psychologist-client); and 35-2-610 (hospital-patient)].	• HMOs may not disclose any enrollee/applicant health information without express consent, except to carry out the purposes of the HMO Act; in a claim or litigation between the person and the HMO; to implement public medical assistance programs; and as required by statute [Wyo. Stat. Ann. § 26-34-130]. • A hospital may not disclose patient health information to any other person without the patient's consent, except to the extent a recipient needs to know the information, if the disclosure is to a person providing health care to the patient; for health care education or for planning, quality assurance, peer review or administrative or other services to the hospital; to immediate family members; or for approved research [Wyo. Stat. Ann. § 35-2-609]. • Specific disclosure rules apply to mental health [Wyo. Stat. Ann. § 25-10-122]; child abuse reports [Wyo. Stat. Ann. § 14-3-214]; and sexually transmitted diseases [Wyo. Stat. Ann. §§ 35-4-107, 35-4-130, 35-4-132].

APPENDIX D: ABC HEALTH CARE SYSTEM PRIVACY POLICIES AND PROCEDURES

Prepared by Clay Countryman at Kean, Miller, d'Armond, McGowan & Jaman, L.L.P. in Baton Rouge, LA

POLICY: Disclosures for Judicial and Administrative Proceedings	
PAGE: 1 of 4	
DATE APPROVED:	EFFECTIVE DATE:

APPLICABLE AREAS: All ABC Health Care System Facilities, Employees, and Agents

PURPOSE: To describe the types of permissible disclosures of Protected Health Information by ABC Health Care System and its affiliated facilities in the course of a judicial or administrative proceeding.

POLICY: Employees and agents of ABC Health Care System and our affiliated providers must make disclosures of Protected Health Information in the course of judicial and administrative proceedings in accordance with all federal and state laws and regulations, specifically including the Privacy Rule promulgated pursuant to the Health Insurance Portability and Accountability Act of 1996.

DEFINITIONS:

(A) **Individually Identifiable Health Information** is information that is a subset of health information, including demographic information collected from an individual, and:

  (1) Is created or received by a health care provider, health plan, employer, or health care clearinghouse; and

  (2) Relates to the past, present, or future physical or mental health or condition of an individual; the provision of health care to an individual; or the past, present, or future payment for the provision of health care to an individual; and

   (i) That identifies the individual; or

   (ii) With respect to which there is a reasonable basis to believe the information can be used to identify the individual.

  (3) **Disclosure** means the release, transfer, provision of access to, or divulging in any other manner of information outside the entity holding the information.

POLICY: Disclosures for Judicial and Administrative Proceedings
PAGE: 2 of 4

DATE APPROVED:	EFFECTIVE DATE:

(4) **Protected health information** means Individually Identifiable Health Information that is transmitted or maintained in any form or medium. Protected health information does not include Individually Identifiable Health Information in: (i) education records covered by the Family Educational Rights and Privacy Act, as amended, 20 U.S.C. 1232g; (ii) records described at 20 U.S.C. 1232g(a)(4)(B)(iv); or (iii) employment records held by a covered entity in its role as employer.

(5) **Covered entity** means:

   (1) A health plan;

   (2) A health care clearinghouse; and

   (3) A health care provider who transmits any health information in electronic form in connection with a transaction covered by the HIPAA Privacy Rule.

PROCEDURE:

This Policy describes the permitted disclosures of Protected Health Information by ABC Health Care System in the course of a judicial or administrative proceeding under the HIPAA Privacy Rule. The Privacy Officer of each facility should confirm operations counsel whether there are any preemption issues with state law in their location.

(1) **Permitted Disclosures in a Judicial or Administrative Proceeding.** ABC Health Care System may disclose Protected Health Information in the course of any judicial or administrative proceeding:

   (a) <u>Court Orders.</u> In response to an order of a court or administrative tribunal, provided that only the Protected Health Information that is expressly authorized by such order is disclosed; or

   (b) <u>Subpoenas, Discovery Requests.</u> In response to a subpoena, discovery request, or other lawful process, that is not accompanied by an order of a court or administrative tribunal, if ABC Health Care System receives:

      (i) Satisfactory assurance, as described in _____, from the party seeking the information that reasonable efforts have been made by such party to ensure that the individual who is the subject of the Protected Health Information that has been requested has been given notice of the request; *or*

POLICY: Disclosures for Judicial and Administrative Proceedings	
PAGE: 3 of 4	
DATE APPROVED:	EFFECTIVE DATE:

- (ii) Satisfactory assurance, as described in this Policy, from the party seeking the information that reasonable efforts have been made by such party to secure a qualified protective order that meets the requirements of this Policy.

(b) **Satisfactory Assurance Without a Qualified Protective Order.** ABC Health Care System shall receive satisfactory assurances from a party seeking Protecting Health Information if ABC Health Care System receives from such party a written statement and accompanying documentation demonstrating that:

- (i) The party requesting such information has made a good faith attempt to provide written notice to the individual (or, if the individual's location is unknown, to mail a notice to the individual's last known address);

- (ii) The notice included sufficient information about the litigation or proceeding in which the Protected Health Information is requested to permit the individual to raise an objection to the court or administrative tribunal; and

- (iii) The time for the individual to raise objections to the court or administrative tribunal has elapsed, and:

    - (a) No objections were filed; or

    - (b) All objections filed by the individual have been resolved by the court or the administrative tribunal and the disclosures being sought are consistent with such resolution.

(c) **Satisfactory Assurance With a Qualified Protective Order.** ABC Health Care System shall receive *satisfactory assurances* from a party seeking Protected Health Information, if ABC Health Care System receives from such party a written statement and accompanying documentation demonstrating that:

- (i) The parties to the dispute giving rise to the request for information have agreed to a qualified protective order and have presented it to the court or administrative tribunal with jurisdiction over the dispute; *or*

- (ii) The party seeking the Protected Health Information has requested a qualified protective order from such court or administrative tribunal.

(d) **Qualified Protective Order.** For purposes of this Policy, a qualified protective order means, with respect to Protected Health Information, an order of a court or of an administrative tribunal or a stipulation by the parties to the litigation or administrative proceeding that:

- (i) Prohibits the parties from using or disclosing the Protected Health Information for any purpose other than the litigation or proceeding for which such information was requested; and

POLICY: Disclosures for Judicial and Administrative Proceedings	
PAGE: 4 of 4	
DATE APPROVED:	EFFECTIVE DATE:

      (ii) Requires the return to the covered entity or destruction of the Protected Health Information (including all copies made) at the end of the litigation or proceeding.

(e) **<u>Disclosures without Satisfactory Assurances.</u>** ABC Health Care System may disclose Protected Health Information in response to a lawful process without receiving satisfactory assurance, if ABC Health Care System makes reasonable efforts to provide notice to the individual sufficient to meet the requirements for disclosures described in this policy without a qualified protective order or to seek a qualified protective order sufficient to meet the requirements of this Policy.

REFERENCES:

45 C.F.R. § 164.512(e)

POLICY:	Disclosures of Patient Health Information about Victims of Abuse, Neglect, or Domestic Violence

PAGE: 1 of 3

DATE APPROVED:	EFFECTIVE DATE:

APPLICABLE AREAS: All ABC Health Care System Facilities, Employees, and Agents

PURPOSE: To describe the permissible disclosures of Protected Health Information by ABC Health Care System and its affiliated facilities about victims of abuse, neglect, or domestic violence.

POLICY: Disclosures of Protected Health Information about victims of abuse, neglect, or domestic violence by employees and agents of ABC Health Care System and our affiliated providers should be made in accordance with this policy and all federal and state laws and regulations, specifically including the Privacy Rule promulgated pursuant to the Health Insurance Portability and Accountability Act of 1996.

DEFINITIONS:

(A) **Individually Identifiable Health Information** is information that is a subset of health information, including demographic information collected from an individual, and:

   (1) Is created or received by a health care provider, health plan, employer, or health care clearinghouse; and

   (2) Relates to the past, present, or future physical or mental health or condition of an individual; the provision of health care to an individual; or the past, present, or future payment for the provision of health care to an individual; and

   (i) That identifies the individual; or

   (ii) With respect to which there is a reasonable basis to believe the information can be used to identify the individual.

POLICY:	Disclosures of Patient Health Information about Victims of Abuse, Neglect, or Domestic Violence
PAGE: 2 of 3	
DATE APPROVED:	EFFECTIVE DATE:

(3) **Disclosure** means the release, transfer, provision of access to, or divulging in any other manner of information outside the entity holding the information.

(4) **Protected health information** means Individually Identifiable Health Information that is transmitted or maintained in any form or medium. Protected Health Information does not include Individually Identifiable Health Information in: (i) education records covered by the Family Educational Rights and Privacy Act, as amended, 20 U.S.C. 1232g; (ii) records described at 20 U.S.C. 1232g(a)(4)(B)(iv); or (iii) employment records held by a covered entity in its role as employer.

(5) **Covered entity** means:

   (1) A health plan.

   (2) A health care clearinghouse.

   (3) A health care provider who transmits any health information in electronic form in connection with a transaction covered by the HIPAA Privacy Rule.

PROCEDURE:

This Policy contains the requirements of the HIPAA Privacy Rule that should be followed by ABC Health Care System and its affiliated providers when making disclosures of Protected Health Information about victims of abuse, neglect, or domestic violence.

(1) **Permitted Disclosures.** Except for reports of child abuse or neglect permitted by this policy, ABC Health Care System and its affiliated entities may disclose Protected Health Information about an individual whom ABC Health Care System reasonably believes to be a victim of abuse, neglect, or domestic violence to a government authority, including a social service or protective services agency, authorized by law to receive reports of abuse, neglect, or domestic violence:

   (a) To the extent the disclosure is required by law and the disclosure complies with the relevant requirements of such law;

   (b) If the individual agrees to the disclosure; or

   (c) To the extent the disclosure is expressly authorized by statute or regulation and:

      (i) The Privacy Officer, in the exercise of professional judgment, believes the disclosure is necessary to prevent serious harm to the individual or other potential victims; or

POLICY:	Disclosures of Patient Health Information about Victims of Abuse, Neglect, or Domestic Violence

| PAGE: 3 of 3 ||

DATE APPROVED:	EFFECTIVE DATE:

    (ii) If the individual is unable to agree because of incapacity, a law enforcement or other public official authorized to receive the report represents that the Protected Health Information for which disclosure is sought is not intended to be used against the individual and that an immediate enforcement activity that depends upon the disclosure would be materially and adversely affected by waiting until the individual is able to agree to the disclosure.

(2) **Informing the individual.** If a disclosure is made pursuant to this policy, ABC Health Care System employees and agents must promptly inform the individual that such a report has been or will be made, except if:

(a) The Privacy Official, in the exercise of professional judgment, believes informing the individual would place the individual at risk of serious harm; or

(b) The Privacy Official would be informing a personal representative, and Privacy Official reasonably believes the personal representative is responsible for the abuse, neglect, or other injury, and that informing such person would not be in the best interests of the individual as determined by the covered entity, in the exercise of professional judgment.

REFERENCES:

45 C.F.R. § 164.512(c)

POLICY: Uses and Disclosures of Patient Health Information for Health Oversight Activities
PAGE: 1 of 3
DATE APPROVED: / EFFECTIVE DATE:

APPLICABLE AREAS: All ABC Health Care System Facilities, Employees, and Agents

PURPOSE: To describe the permitted uses and disclosures of Protected Health Information by ABC Health Care System and its affiliated facilities for health oversight activities.

POLICY: Uses and disclosures of Protected Health Information for health oversight activities by employees and agents of ABC Health Care System and our affiliated providers should be in accordance with this policy and all federal and state laws and regulations, specifically including the Privacy Rule promulgated pursuant to the Health Insurance Portability and Accountability Act of 1996.

DEFINITIONS:

(A) **Individually Identifiable Health Information** is information that is a subset of health information, including demographic information collected from an individual, and:

   (1) Is created or received by a health care provider, health plan, employer, or health care clearinghouse; and

   (2) Relates to the past, present, or future physical or mental health or condition of an individual; the provision of health care to an individual; or the past, present, or future payment for the provision of health care to an individual; and

      (i) That identifies the individual; or

      (ii) With respect to which there is a reasonable basis to believe the information can be used to identify the individual.

POLICY: Uses and Disclosures of Patient Health Information for Health Oversight Activities
PAGE: 2 of 3

DATE APPROVED:	EFFECTIVE DATE:

(3) **Disclosure** means the release, transfer, provision of access to, or divulging in any other manner of information outside the entity holding the information.

(4) **Protected health information** means Individually Identifiable Health Information that is transmitted or maintained in any form or medium. Protected Health Information does not include Individually Identifiable Health Information in: (i) education records covered by the Family Educational Rights and Privacy Act, as amended, 20 U.S.C. 1232g; (ii) records described at 20 U.S.C. 1232g(a)(4)(B)(iv); or (iii) employment records held by a covered entity in its role as employer.

(5) **Covered entity** means:

    (1) A health plan.

    (2) A health care clearinghouse.

    (3) A health care provider who transmits any health information in electronic form in connection with a transaction covered by the HIPAA Privacy Rule.

PROCEDURE:

This Policy contains the requirements of the HIPAA Privacy Rule that must be followed when making uses and disclosures of Protected Health Information for health oversight activities.

(1) **Permitted Disclosures.** ABC Health Care System may disclose Protected Health Information to a health oversight agency for oversight activities authorized by law, including audits; civil, administrative, or criminal investigations; inspections; licensure or disciplinary actions; civil, administrative, or criminal proceedings or actions; or other activities necessary for appropriate oversight of:

(a) The health care system;

(b) Government benefit programs for which health information is relevant to beneficiary eligibility;

(c) Entities subject to government regulatory programs for which health information is necessary for determining compliance with program standards; or

(d) Entities subject to civil rights laws for which health information is necessary for determining compliance.

POLICY: Uses and Disclosures of Patient Health Information for Health Oversight Activities
PAGE: 3 of 3

DATE APPROVED:	EFFECTIVE DATE:

(2) **Disclosures that Are Not Considered for Health Oversight Activities.** For the purpose of the disclosures permitted by paragraph (A) above, a health oversight activity does not include an investigation or other activity in which the individual is the subject of the investigation or activity and such investigation or other activity does not arise out of and is not directly related to:

(a) The receipt of health care;

(b) A claim for public benefits related to health; or

(c) Qualification for, or receipt of, public benefits or services when a patient's health is integral to the claim for public benefits or services.

(3) **Joint Activities or Investigations.** If a health oversight activity or investigation is conducted in conjunction with an oversight activity or investigation relating to a claim for public benefits not related to health, the joint activity or investigation is considered a health oversight activity for purposes of this Policy.

REFERENCES:

45 C.F.R. § 164.512(d)

About the Author

PATRICIA I. CARTER, J.D. advises health care providers on HIPAA and other privacy/confidentiality laws, Medicare and Medicaid reimbursement rules, provider licensing, compliance programs, medical staff issues, provider contracting, and other regulatory and business matters. In addition, she advises employers and health plans on ERISA, HIPAA, and other health plan and benefits issues. Prior to becoming an attorney, Ms. Carter had a successful 14-year career in health plan administration, including 10 years as an information systems manager, trainer, and consultant for health plan administrators.

Ms. Carter is a frequent lecturer and writer on the HIPAA privacy and security regulations and speaks at national conferences on these topics. Her published articles include "Applying your Corporate Compliance Skills to the HIPAA Security Standards," in the *Journal of Health Information Management*; "Health Information Privacy: Can Congress Protect Confidential Medical Information in the Information Age?" in the *William Mitchell Law Review*, and "Telemedicine in Minnesota: A Primer for Physicians," in *Minnesota Medicine*.

Ms. Carter received her J.D., *magna cum laude*, from Hamline University School of Law, and her B.A., *magna cum laude*, from the University of Minnesota.

Ms. Carter is an attorney with the law firm of Gray, Plant, Mooty, Mooty & Bennett, P.A., in Minneapolis, Minnesota and is a member of the firm's Health Law Practice Group. She can be reached at *patricia.carter@gpmlaw.com*, at 612-343-2800, or through the firm's Web site at *www.gpmlaw.com*.